Throwing it All Away

Blissful
Beings

Throwing It All Away

A Son's Suicide and a Mother's Search for Hope

BY NINA OWEN

Throwing It All Away
Copyright © 2020 by Nina Owen

Published by
Southern Fried Karma, LLC
Atlanta, GA
www.sfkpress.com

Books are available in quantity for promotional or premium use. For information, email pr@sfkmultimedia.com.

This is a work of nonfiction. Some names and identifying details have been changed to protect the privacy of individuals.

ISBN: 978-1-970137-02-6
eISBN: 978-1-970137-03-3
Library of Congress Control Number: Pending

Cover design by Olivia Croom Hammerman
Cover art by maradon 333 on Shutterstock.com
Interior by Vinnie Kinsella

Printed in the United States of America.

This book is lovingly dedicated to my husband, Jeff, and our children—Sam, Maggie, and Claire. Family is forever.

Contents

So sorry to be leaving in such an abrupt manner, but it really is time that I get going. I've greatly overstayed my welcome on this world. Whether or not you agree with me, I find a serene beauty in throwing it all away.

Sam

Preface

This is the true story of a profoundly tragic event that took place in my family in 2016. To the best of my ability, I have been as truthful and honest with the reader as I am with myself, striving to present my son, my family, and myself as we were and are.

Direct passages, written in Sam's voice, are copied verbatim from his notes, emails, texts, high school assignments, documents from his computer, and journals he kept. I feel fortunate to have uncovered my son's written records. Along with many other gifts, he was a good, self-reflective writer.

My voice is my unvarnished truth. Composing this memoir has deepened my knowledge of my son, which has only increased my appreciation of, pride in, and love for him. One thing this book did not do was heal me from the loss of Sam. I will never be completely whole again.

No family is perfect, and indeed ours is not. However, Jeff and I did all we knew to do to raise our children in a happy and secure home. We have always told our kids there would be nothing they could do to make us not love them or to make us abandon them. Family is forever.

I spend a lot of time in this book talking about how remarkable Sam was, but my daughters, Maggie and Claire, are equally remarkable. I could make long lists and even write books about each of these beautiful girls's fabulous traits and their impacts on others. My love for them and pride in them is second to none. They are my reasons to live. This book, however, is Sam's story.

In Woody Allen's movie *Midnight in Paris*, the character of Ernest Hemingway says, "No subject is terrible if the story is true, if the prose is clean and honest, and if it affirms courage and grace under pressure."

I'm not sure that I have exhibited grace under pressure, but it has taken great courage for me to talk about my son's depression and drug use, his struggle to get well, his death, my indescribable grief and overwhelming guilt, and the life-changing metaphysical spiritual journey I underwent after Sam's death.

Although my spiritual awakening may not ring true to what you believe or what your religion teaches, my account is factual—everything recorded did indeed occur.

In the beginning, I was terrified to share my story. But once I found Sam's written documents, I felt compelled to relay it. If by telling our story even one life is saved, the pain of divulging such personal information will have been worth it. My prayer is that this book will save a life and, therefore, a family.

I hope this book shows how the loss of one life ripples through a family and a community, leaving a sense of helplessness and hopelessness in its wake. Suicide is not always planned; it can be an impulsive act and, with the right help, can be averted. I hope you will read this memoir with an open mind and an open heart. If this could happen to my family, it could happen to anyone's.

PART I

LOSING SAM

"Sadly enough, the most painful goodbyes are the ones that are left unsaid and never explained."

—JONATHAN HARNISCH

CHAPTER 1

A Wretched Twenty-Four Hours

S tarting my mornings with a ritual helps keep me sane. For years, I've always gotten regular morning exercise four to five days a week.

The morning of February 25, 2016, a Thursday, started like hundreds of other mornings for me. I woke at seven and, still in my pajamas, went downstairs for my morning coffee. My husband, Jeff, had left for work, and I could smell the coffee already made. I placed my hand on the side of the stainless-steel coffee pot, making sure it was still warm, and chose a cup from the cabinet and filled it. I added a drizzle of half and half to my mug before going back upstairs to dress for a run.

The weather app on my phone said it was 42 degrees with clear skies. I pulled on my black running tights, a long-sleeved blue dry-fit shirt, and a white polar fleece vest.

At 7:15, I walked out my front door and up the cul-de-sac toward the house kitty-cornered from mine, where my friend Angela lived. The houses on my street, just thirteen of them, all have a similar brick façade on the front, with wood siding on the other three sides. Our neighborhood contains over a thousand homes, all maintained by the same strict HOA guidelines enforcing a bizarre uniformity.

As I stood in Angela's driveway waiting for her, I shivered and pulled the ends of my sleeves down to cover my hands. She came out of her house, dressed in an outfit nearly matching mine, her dark hair pulled back in a loose ponytail in preparation for our thrice-weekly run.

We walked down our street toward the main road that intersects our neighborhood, me—as always—on Angela's left side. We had been running together for thirteen years, and if I ever ended up on her right side, we both felt like something was askew.

"What's new?" she asked.

"Oh, you know, the usual—I'm worried about Sam."

Angela was used to me talking about Sam, or any other personal concern. She had two children herself, ages 15 and 18, and I never felt judged by her, a valuable and too-rare asset in adult friendship. Angela checked all the boxes of being a good friend—trustworthiness, honesty, dependability, empathy, and loyalty. She was a welcome ear I relied on to feel sane and grounded. As we began to run, Angela asked me what was going on with Sam.

"He's going to break up with Hannah, but he's feeling anxious about the fallout," I said, referring to his girlfriend of the last three months, one I thought brought unnecessary—and unhelpful—drama to his life. I confided in Angela that Sam had told me the night before that Hannah was making threats about hurting herself if he ended their relationship. When he hadn't reacted the way she'd wanted, she'd told him that her parents had kicked her out of their house and she had nowhere to go. Suspicious, I'd texted her mom, and I'd learned they hadn't kicked her out.

"That girl sounds deeply troubled," Angela said. We both agreed that continuing a relationship with her was not what Sam, who had been suffering from major depressive disorder over the last six months, needed. Even so, we both knew from our own experiences of early relationships that it was going to be tough on Sam after the breakup. He'd have to adjust to not having a girlfriend around all the time, and I knew I would need to keep an eye on him. Sam was getting treatment for his depression and lately seemed happier and more positive. Still, I worried that this big shift in his social life would be a hit to his fragile psyche.

"I think having something for Sam to look forward to would help him adjust to being without Hannah," Angela offered.

I wondered aloud if Sam had any plans for his spring break, which was a couple of weeks away.

"I just thought of something," I said. "I'm going to a Hilton national conference in Dallas in March. I think it's the same time as Sam's spring break. Maybe I should ask him to go with me. I'm pretty sure he has a friend who is doing an internship in Dallas this semester."

Sam had started back at Georgia Institute of Technology in January, after taking a leave of absence the previous semester. He was majoring in physics, and he was taking a modest load of three classes this semester and living at home. Back in December, I had asked Angela her opinion on Sam restarting school on a part-time basis, and she had thought that had been a good plan. The other options had been for Sam to either take another semester off from school or to start back full-time and live on campus. With Sam's agreement, we had decided that easing back in was the best idea.

After our 45-minute run, Angela and I parted. I entered my house and went directly downstairs to Sam's bedroom in the basement. I felt a heart-tugging need to check on him. Looking back, I can't say I know why this need was so strong, but I knew I wanted to see him.

When I walked into Sam's room, he was lying on his stomach in bed, shirtless, still sleeping. His long arms were thrown over his head and his thick brown hair seemed to be sticking out in all directions. The rumpled sheets and quilt were pulled up to his waist. I paused and looked at him a moment—my little boy had turned into a 20-year-old man. How had that happened so quickly? I inhaled sharply, but the exhale caught in my throat. *God, I love this kid.*

"Sam?"

He sat up abruptly, turned to face me, and urgently asked, "What time is it?"

"Just past eight."

Rather than responding, he looked at me expectantly, probably wondering why I was in his room. Sam needed to go to Suwanee Municipal Court later in the day to attend traffic court and pay a speeding fine. After that, he planned to go to his part-time job delivering pizzas. He didn't have class that day.

I proposed the trip to Dallas, saying I could upgrade my hotel room to a two-room suite and use miles to get him an airline ticket. I suggested he could hang out with his friend doing the internship there.

Sam's demeanor was solemn, but that was not out of the ordinary for him. I tried to remember the last time I had heard him laugh out loud. His eyes were a little hooded, and I wondered if he had gotten much sleep the night before.

"Yeah, that might work," he said with a nod, looking directly into my eyes. With that statement, he seemed finished with our conversation, and I went upstairs to shower.

By 9:00, I was in my home office, working at my job in hotel operations. Although my office is on the main floor of the house, it's in the back, and so as I worked that morning, I didn't have a view of our front yard or driveway.

I quickly became immersed in a flood of emails and phone calls, my awareness of the hustle and hum of the house around me receding. Around one in the afternoon, I heard the click of the front door opening. My thirteen-year-old daughter, Claire, came in. It was an early-release day at her middle school, and she had ridden the bus home.

I greeted her at the door. "How was your day?" I asked.

"It was fine. What's there to eat?" I'd learned to expect this sort of response to my questions. I longed for the elementary-school days when my kids would come home and excitedly tell me about their day. Claire, my youngest, had only been thirteen for a month, but she was already falling into that teenage mode of not wanting to share with me.

I listed off the snacks we had on hand—popcorn, apples, yogurt—before returning to my office. Another twenty minutes passed, and then I heard Sam's solid footfalls coming up the basement steps. He went out without saying anything, shutting the front door hard.

Our three-year-old white Great Pyrenees/Labrador mix, Sadie, usually spends most of her day keeping guard in the foyer or the dining room—barking to alert me of a UPS truck or other strange vehicle on our street. But on this day, she stayed in my office, lying on the rug. If I got up and went to another part of the house, Sadie would not leave my side. She wouldn't eat and wouldn't go outside. I thought this odd enough to send a text to Jeff and the kids, telling them I thought Sadie might be sick or depressed. My husband and both of our girls—Maggie, our fifteen-year-old, and Claire—responded, but Sam, I noticed, didn't. I continued working. Maggie came home from school at her usual 3:00, the sound of the front door once again prompting me to look up from my computer screen. I greeted her as I had with Claire and asked how her day had been. I received a similarly noncommittal response. Teenagers.

I continued to field phone calls and review sales reports from the twenty-five salespeople who reported to me until 3:30, at which time I began to have a vague sense of anxiety about Sam—a familiar feeling from the last six months. I could not pinpoint the exact reason I was feeling this way, other than that I knew he was resentful about the speeding fine, which was over $200, and anxious about Hannah. I called him.

The call went straight to voicemail, so I sent a text: "Everything go okay in traffic court?"

No response.

I called Jeff to see if he'd heard from Sam. He hadn't, but he said he'd text him. Jeff's text also went unanswered. I tried calling Sam again, thinking he might answer this time, but he didn't.

I felt my heartbeat quicken. I was starting to worry. My worry was not misplaced; Sam had overdosed in his dorm room at Georgia Tech in September. We had spent the months since getting him treatment. I called Jeff back and asked if he would come home early from work. He said he would try.

Around 5:30, Andy, Sam's boss at the pizza place, texted me looking for Sam. I've known Andy and his wife, Courtney, for years. They live in our neighborhood, and, like us, are a tennis and swim team family. In his text, Andy said Sam had texted him that afternoon at 12:50 p.m. saying he could be at work at 4:00, but he had not shown up and wasn't answering his phone. I texted back that I hadn't been able to get in touch with him either and was worried. Andy said he would reach out to the other delivery guys to see if they'd heard from him.

Jeff was now home. When I told him about my conversation with Andy, I could tell he was starting to get concerned. Nevertheless, trying to reassure me that Sam was okay, he called Verizon, but the cellphone service could not pick up a ping to locate Sam. My stomach dropped.

The time had come to call Hannah. I had been reluctant to call her, not sure if she and Sam had already broken up. I dialed her number anyway and told her we could not locate Sam. Her response was, "Oh, he really *is* missing?" I had no idea what that meant until she said she hadn't been able to connect with him all day. I kept the phone call short and asked her to keep trying.

Jeff and I made a list of Sam's friends and divided it down the middle. I began calling and texting one set while Jeff took the other. After an hour of this without success, I went downstairs to the basement, looking for any clues that might help us find him. I observed his rumpled bedsheets, his clothes on the floor, and his laptop inside a backpack on top of the bed. As a child and teen, Sam had always been neat and kept his room in order. This sloppiness was relatively new. I opened the laptop and moved the touchpad; the screen lit up but requested a password I didn't know.

Sam's desk held a monitor and keyboard for a gaming computer he had built when he'd been fourteen. It, too, was password protected. Next to the keyboard was a red spiral notebook opened to a page filled with his firm, tight script: a pros-and-cons list regarding breaking up with Hannah. Sam, always logical, was prone to analyzing situations, but this was the first pros-and-cons list I'd witnessed from him. I looked it over but didn't see anything specifically alarming. Searching his bathroom and the basement media room proved similarly fruitless. Back upstairs, I texted Sam again.

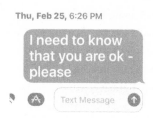

Thu, Feb 25, 6:26 PM

I need to know that you are ok - please

Text Message

JEFF AND I resumed making calls. We called and texted any friend of Sam's we could think of—Todd, Dan, Adam, Jackson, Nabeel, Dhroov, Michael, Will, Ibrahim. Sam had a large friend group from a variety of things—high school, college, swim team, and work. Todd and Jackson had been Sam's friends since second grade. No one had heard from him that day. An ad hoc phone tree fanned out—each friend began trying to get in touch with Sam and contacting anyone they knew who might know his whereabouts. Some posted missing notices on social media.

Hannah called Jeff back and said she knew Sam's computer login for his laptop; Jeff logged in to it. He looked through Sam's documents and email but didn't see anything alarming. Neither of us thought of checking his Google search history.

Hannah said she and her mother would call all the hospitals in greater Atlanta to see if he had been admitted. I agreed this was a good—yet terrifying—idea. Every conversation with Hannah spiked my anxiety. What did she know that she was not telling us?

Since Sam's bank account was tied to mine, I logged in to look at his recent purchases; there had been no transactions that day. One of Sam's friends called me and suggested we check his Bitcoin account. At the time, I didn't even know what that was. Again, it was password-protected. Jeff researched and found a phone number for Bitcoin. His call there was a maddening dead-end. They would offer no assistance in letting us check our son's account. Jeff, normally good-natured, hung up on the call center worker.

One friend said he would search for Sam on campus and advised us to alert the Georgia Tech Police Department. Before I could make that call, Sam's dean, the Dean of Sciences at the university, called me. He had heard that Sam was missing and said he would immediately get the GTPD involved in searching for him. At each dead end, I could feel the walls closing in tighter. No one was saying anything to give me hope. My fear made it hard to breathe deeply or see or speak clearly.

Our daughters knew we were looking for Sam, but they mostly stood to the side as we continued our electronic search. Jeff and I checked on them periodically, but they told us they didn't need anything. Maggie and Claire must have made their own dinner that night. I don't remember.

We tried calling the Suwanee Municipal Court to learn whether he had shown up to pay his speeding fine, but they had left for the day. I told Jeff that I had an awful feeling and wanted to involve the police. Jeff called the Gwinnett County Police Department to file a missing person's report.

Around 9:00 that night, a deputy came to our house to collect information for the report. He was tall and dressed in uniform, the usual badges on his shirt front and patches along his sleeves. On his left shoulder, he wore a squawking walky-talky. I wondered why he had brought in the walky-talky. Who would he need to talk to? As he entered, he removed his broad-brimmed hat and muted the device.

The three of us stood in the foyer. I'm not sure whether we asked him to sit and he declined or whether, in our frenzied state, we neglected to ask him into our family room. Either way, we all stood near the front door as Jeff gave the deputy Sam's picture and a full description. I told the deputy what we had done and where we had searched. He nodded curtly, leaving me feeling a bit insignificant. Jeff told the officer that Sam was under psychiatric care and had tried to kill himself once before. The officer told us that even though Sam was over eighteen, there was a way—a complicated multi-step process—that we could hospitalize him without his consent, and that we should research this. *But first we need to find him,* I thought.

The officer left, saying he would be in touch. For a minute or more, Jeff and I stood numbly in our spots in the foyer, too frightened to speak. I believe we both felt that by speaking our fears out loud, that would make them more real.

I walked into the family room and sat on one end of the sofa. Jeff was still in the foyer when the girls came downstairs to ask tentative questions. I couldn't hear their questions, nor his responses. Given my puffy eyes and expression of despair, they must not have wanted to approach me. Not long after, they went to bed.

Jeff and I also went upstairs to our bedroom. He undressed and got into bed.

"How can you possibly sleep when Sam is missing?" I asked.

"Well, what more can I do right now? Staying up worrying won't help find him."

"Going to bed is like giving up!"

"I'm not giving up; I think he is okay, and we'll hear from him soon."

I looked at Jeff, wishing and trying to catch even a glimmer of the hope he still had. But I couldn't. In frustration, I left the room.

As Jeff slept, I paced the house. I spoke aloud—praying, I guess—saying only "Please God. Please God. Please don't take Sam. Let him be okay." Into the wee hours, I replied to texts from Andy and others concerned for Sam. I pricked up at any sound, anxious to hear Sam's car coming into the driveway—willing to hear the thumping bass of his stereo signaling his arrival. Around three in the morning, I lay down on top of the covers, next to Jeff. I had not intended to sleep, but my exhaustion overtook my will, and I dozed off.

I woke at 5:30 a.m., bolting upright. *How could I have possibly fallen asleep?* I felt dizzy and lightheaded, my heart in my throat and my entire body clenched tight. I ran to the front window, hoping to see Sam's car. Although it was still dark outside, the streetlights illuminated the front of our house. Our concrete driveway was empty. My heart dropped even further. Frightened but refusing to give up, I grabbed my phone and again tried to reach him.

That morning, we told Maggie and Claire they had the option of staying home from school. Maggie, a sophomore in high school, chose to stay home, realizing the gravity of our family's situation. Claire, who was in seventh grade, said she'd instead go to school to keep herself distracted.

Trying to sound optimistic, we told them we would let them know when Sam was found. I sent a group text to my parents, brothers, and sister to tell them what was going on. In my text, I asked that they text back and not call. I think I did this because I was scared to hear the fear in their voices.

At 8:00 a.m., Jeff and I got into our minivan and drove through Suwanee, hoping to find Sam's dark red Mazda 3 parked on a side street or in a parking lot. We were at Suwanee Municipal Court as soon as it opened at 8:30, to ask whether Sam had shown up for traffic court the day before.

The woman at the front desk looked up Sam's name and told us he hadn't been there. In a manner meant to calm us—she must have assumed we were only worried that Sam would be in trouble for not showing up for his appointment—she said, "It's fine. There is another date he can come and pay the fine. Just tell him to get in touch with me." She gave us her card.

The Suwanee Police Department was one building over, and Jeff and I went there next. Even though we didn't live in the Suwanee city limits, the policeman at the desk listened, concerned. Technically the city police had no jurisdiction over us; that was why we had filed the missing person's report with a county officer the night before. But we were hoping they would help. The officer took our information and asked for Sam's picture. I began to fumble through my iPhone, but I was shaking so uncontrollably that I could not work the device. Instead, Jeff found a picture on his phone and emailed it to the department. The officer said he would distribute the information to the force and they would be on the lookout. He advised us to look for Sam's car at the hotels near our exit on I-85, as they had in the past found missing people there, checked into rooms, drunk or high.

Jeff and I got back into our van and drove the short distance to the access road lined with economy hotels: Motel 6, Super 8, Red Roof Inn. In my fifteen years in Suwanee, I had never been down this road. I found it hard to believe that Sam could be in one of these places, but I desperately wanted him to be. We drove slowly through every parking lot, looking for his car. I feverishly hoped that maybe Sam was just high—perhaps he needed to get to a hospital but was alive. *God, please, he must be okay!* I thought. I was beyond *asking* God to help us. Now I was making demands. As Jeff made turns around the corners of each hotel building, I held my breath and willed Sam's car to appear. It didn't.

We drove to the parks and greenway parking lots in Suwanee. Hannah had suggested this, saying they hung out at parks all the time. Again, I reasoned with God. Again, there was no sign of Sam or his car. It was late morning now. More than 20 hours had passed since anyone had spoken with Sam. I texted him again. "Sam, please get in touch with Dad or me," I wrote, hands shaking. "You cannot imagine how desperate we feel."

Jeff looked over to me. "Why are you still texting him? His phone is off!"

"But there's a chance he could have turned it back on," I countered.

Jeff and I were feeding off each other's anxiety. The hope that Jeff had still harbored when he'd gone to bed the night before seemed to have dissipated. A strained silence fell between us.

AROUND NOON, WE were still driving around Gwinnett County when Hannah called Jeff to say there was a post on Reddit that someone had just killed himself by jumping from a building in Midtown Atlanta. She seemed convinced it could be Sam.

"Start driving into Atlanta," I urged Jeff.

"Nina, we don't even know where to go!"

"Just drive!" I screamed.

As Jeff drove south on I-85, I made phone calls to the police precincts near Georgia Tech. After two dead ends, I finally reached the right precinct and explained that my son was missing and I wanted to make sure he was not the person who had jumped from the roof of a building in the city. The policeman asked Sam's name and said that was not the name of the deceased. I asked a second time to verify. It was not Sam. I thanked the officer.

"It's not him," I said to Jeff.

He and I both trembled with cautious relief. We turned in the direction of home. At least for now, we could continue to hope.

CHAPTER 2

The Early Years

When I was in high school in the early 1980s, I told anyone who asked that I never wanted children. What I most wanted was a career as a newspaper journalist, I told them with practiced rhetoric. I wanted the flexibility to travel. I wanted to marry but, being both a feminist and a moderate liberal for as long as I can remember, I loved saying this was my choice to make. One does not have to marry and then procreate to be happy.

This was what I told people. But, in my deepest self, I knew that part of the reason for not wanting children was my own unhappy adolescence, during most of which I felt unattractive and unloved. My depression began with menarche at age eleven and lasted into my twenties. During my teens, I remember having nights when I would cry so hard that my eyes would be puffy all the next day. If you'd asked me what was wrong, I doubt I could have told you. My depression was a heaviness in my soul. At a young age, I remember thinking that my great-grandmother was the lucky one because she had her life behind her rather than in front of her. The life in front of me seemed impossibly hard.

I did not want a child to have to live through the same level of sadness and despair. It seemed cruel for me to pass on a predisposition for adolescent depression. But after getting married, I could not really put voice to why I would ever have said that I did not want a baby. My depression was that much at bay. Yes, adolescence and early adulthood had been rocky for me, but I had survived, right? I was sure that I would offer my child or children every advantage and any needed support or intervention, should they also go through depression. But, really, why worry? I told myself I would have only perfect children—intelligent, confident, beautiful, loving—and not only would they be perfect, Jeff and I would be perfect parents: patient, nurturing, giving, loving, compassionate, and very involved. *Yep, we can do this!* Ah, young parents' naiveté and capacity for hope...

Jeff and I started trying to conceive in August 1994, a little over a year after we'd married and a little more than two after we'd first met. After only a month of trying, it happened. We were thrilled and told everyone we knew right away, despite the usual protocol of waiting until the second trimester. I immediately began to buy maternity clothes, and Jeff and I spent a weekend or two looking at cribs and planning a nursery. My initial doctor visits were uneventful. All was going according to plan.

On the afternoon of November 11, I was working in my office at the Northeast Atlanta Hilton. During a bathroom break, I saw blood. A lot. I was thirteen weeks pregnant. I walked back to my office and shakily dialed Jeff's number. "It's me," I said when he picked up. "Something's wrong; I'm bleeding."

Jeff sounded distracted with his work. "Oh. I bet everything is fine," he said. "Call your doctor and let me know what she says." Jeff has always been the optimist in our relationship. Sometimes that optimism is contagious. This time it fell flat.

I hung up the phone and called my obstetrician's office. The nurse I spoke with also tried to reassure me but asked that I come into the office right away. I called Jeff back and asked if he would meet me there. He apologized and said he had a meeting. "Call me when you get to the office and get checked out." This statement stung a bit. I wanted the baby and me to be his primary concern. I didn't communicate it with him, but I had an instinct that something was wrong.

At the doctor's office, the nurse took my blood pressure. It was abnormally high. She asked if I was nervous, and I gave her a tight nod. I followed her into the exam room and lay down on the examination table as instructed. Minutes later, the doctor walked briskly into the room. I wondered if she thought I was an overly paranoid first-time expectant mother, wasting her time.

Using a handheld Doppler device, the doctor searched for the baby's heartbeat. The only heartbeat we could hear was mine. She continued to move the apparatus across my entire abdomen. I looked at her face for any sign of encouragement. There was none. Tears slipped from the corners of my eyes, down my cheeks, and into my ears.

"Hang on," she said, "I'm going to use a vaginal ultrasound." As she walked out of the examination room, my breath caught in my throat. *Is this sort of thing normal?* I wondered but was afraid to ask. The nurse had me scoot farther down the table and place my feet in stirrups. The doctor came back in, wheeling the ultrasound machine. After several minutes of looking inside my uterus for any sign of life, the doctor shook her head.

"Mrs. Owen, I'm sorry."

I rose to a sitting position and cried out. I couldn't catch my breath. When the nurse asked my husband's phone number, I could barely get the digits out of my mouth. The doctor's office was only ten minutes from our house, so I drove myself home. Jeff met me there, and we sat on our sofa, his arm around my shoulders while I cried. We had already begun to love this child. This was a terrible blow to both of us.

Because this was a "missed miscarriage," I had to have a dilation and curettage operation, a D&C, two days later to remove any tissue from my uterus. After the procedure, the doctor told me I should wait three months before getting pregnant again. I made it two months. In January, the doctor confirmed the second pregnancy. Because I hadn't waited the required time, she was concerned and prescribed a progesterone supplement for me to take the first three months of my pregnancy.

It worked, and after nine months—and thirteen hours of labor—Sam was born at 11:20 p.m., October 22, 1995. My first sight of him was a headful of dark brown hair and scrunched eyes fighting to open against the glaring lights. After he was bathed, measured, and weighed—eight pounds, two ounces; 22 inches long—he was handed to me swathed in a Northside Hospital blanket, white with blue and pink pinstripes.

As I looked at him, I took note of his long, dark eyelashes lying atop his cheek bones. I had never seen such a thing on a newborn. He opened his eyes—not my blue nor my husband's chocolate brown, but something in between. A lighter brown with a hint of gold sparkle—hazel, I guess, but that description did not do his eyes justice. I looked at his sweet face and immediately felt like I already knew him; without a doubt, we were meant to be mom and son.

Along with being overjoyed, I also felt overwhelmed. I questioned my ability to care for this fragile creature. What if I dropped him? What if I didn't know how to soothe him? What had I gotten myself into? Nursing was a problem for the first weeks. I visited a lactation nurse because I couldn't figure out how to get Sam to latch on properly. Then I came down with a raging case of mastitis, realizing its severity only when my fever spiked to 104 degrees. But I didn't give up. While I was recovering from mastitis, I pumped breast milk to bottle-feed Sam. After some time, I healed, and Sam and I got settled into a comfortable routine of nursing. In fact, after a couple of months, he refused to take a bottle. He was so stubborn about this that when I weaned him at nine months, I weaned him to a sippy cup.

WHEN SAM WAS born, the plan was that I would take a three-month maternity leave and then return to work, putting Sam in a daycare. I remember the exact moment I knew I could not leave him to some stranger's care. I was sitting in a rocking chair in his nursery, holding him. I looked at his face and thought, *How can I possibly put him in a place where he won't be held enough or loved enough—a place where several babies will be vying for the attention of one or two daycare workers?* No one would ever love Sam as much as I would, and no one could take better care of him. Jeff was in full support of my decision to quit my job and stay home with Sam, taking part-time freelance work on the side. I loved being home with Sam. I was completely consumed by this sweet baby. Jeff and I were in love with him beyond anything we had thought we could feel.

SAM HAD AN innate ability to learn quickly, and I was an attentive teacher. At seventeen months, he could recognize and recite each letter of the alphabet, and his vocabulary grew every day. He would always ask questions, but usually just once. He would immediately absorb the new knowledge.

Sam frequently went through phases of complete enthrallment with different subjects. At the ages of two and three, it was cars, trains, trucks, and planes. At four, he became fascinated with dinosaurs. I was told by his friend Katie that when they were at high school parties, Sam used his knowledge of dinosaurs as a party trick, reciting little-known facts about each species. I laughed when Katie told me this; I could see him doing such a thing.

As Sam grew older, he became consumed with another passion: putting together Lego sets. He would put a kit together following the instructions once (usually on Christmas Day or the day after his birthday), but then tear it apart and create something brand new. His creations of racecars and airplanes and buildings were sometimes as inventive and well-built as the ones from the instructions.

When Sam was in second grade, he gave himself a haircut, as many young children do. In Sam's case, he used some old clippers to give himself the beginnings of a "reverse mohawk." The clippers were the same ones Jeff's dad—a Navy veteran—had used on Jeff as a child. They had been stored in our downstairs bathroom cabinet. Luckily, Sam's hair was especially thick, and he got only a few inches from his forehead before the clippers clogged. When I asked Sam why he would do such a thing, he dissolved into laughter. Didn't I see how hysterical a reverse mohawk was? How his friends would love it? I still have a copy of his class photo from that year, with Sam proudly displaying a patchy growth of hair above his forehead. I don't think I shared that picture with the relatives.

In 1998, Sam and I were on a flight home from Memphis that got caught in severe weather from a tornado. Though he was not yet three years old, he appeared calmer than a seasoned traveler. I've always been prone to motion sickness, and while the plane lurched and I choked back my nausea, Sam sat stoically, seeming to know he had to help Mom through this. The kid was an old soul and my most efficient consoler.

Eight years later, when Sam was in fifth grade, I took him on an American Council for International Studies youth educational tour of France. Our group leader, Ms. Elene, was one of my mother-in-law's dearest friends. Ms. Elene taught seventh-grade French at a private school in Anniston, Alabama. Members of her class and their parents traveled with us.

The first time I had been abroad had been on my honeymoon, so I jumped at the chance to take eleven-year-old Sam to Europe. I thought making this special trip together would strengthen our bond. As a child in a family of five kids, I had never had the opportunity to take a trip with one of my parents. I wanted this vacation to be a special memory that Sam would have for the rest of his life.

The trip was in mid-March, just a little early for "Springtime in Paris." The weather was mostly cold and wet, but we made the best of it. We spent time in Paris, Normandy, and the Loire Valley. I enjoyed being one-on-one with Sam. He wanted to learn everything he could. In anticipation of the trip to the D-Day beaches, Sam and I had watched *Saving Private Ryan*. He loved Normandy and hearing about the war. In Paris, the only tours I think he didn't care for were the several cathedrals. After all, how much can an eleven-year-old boy appreciate flying buttresses? One evening, as part of a wonderful five-course meal at an upscale restaurant in Paris, we were served a decadent, beautifully plated dessert with chocolate ganache and raspberries. Sam love the dessert—so much that, after he had consumed every bite, he picked up his plate and licked it! I was horrified and embarrassed, but when Ms. Elene laughed aloud, I reminded myself that he was still a young boy. Sam's maturity beyond his years made it easy to forget.

In another memory, Sam was about two, and I was reading a book to him in our family room. I told him I was going upstairs to brush my teeth and would be back down in "a jiff." I went upstairs, brushed my teeth, changed out of my pajamas, and went back downstairs, only to find that Sam was no longer in the family room. I checked our kitchen and other downstairs rooms. He wasn't there.

Our dog, Abby, was barking excitedly, and I wondered if Sam had wandered onto our outside deck. Suddenly (and nonsensically), I remembered that a child had been abducted in a carjacking at a gas station near us the week before. Had someone taken him?! I began to yell for Sam. I went up and down the stairs, checking everywhere for him. I dialed my neighbor to help me search, and just as she picked up the phone, I heard a noise from behind our oak entertainment center. There, squeezed in with the wires and cables, was my toddler.

"Peek-boo," he said with a big smile.

I didn't know whether to cry or laugh or scold. I told my neighbor that all was fine and hugged that little kid hard.

"Sam, do not ever do that to Mommy again!"

AFTER SUFFERING TWO additional miscarriages, one when Sam was two-and-a-half and the other when he was three, Jeff and I eventually welcomed a second child—a daughter, Maggie—into the world. Jeff and I felt tremendous love for and pride in our beautiful daughter. What a wonderful blessing she was.

Just before Maggie was born, in July 2000, we moved from our neighborhood in Alpharetta to Suwanee. Our Alpharetta home was in a small neighborhood of only 100 homes. By then, Sam was four, and I wanted to move to a community where our young family could participate in swim team, tennis team, and community events.

We found a home in Morning View—a subdivision holding over a thousand homes. The move to such a large neighborhood was not necessarily our intention, but we found a house we liked with the amenities we were looking for there. We had left good neighbors and playmates for Sam in our old neighborhood, and I was nervous about how that would play out in the new place. We moved on the Fourth of July weekend, exactly one month before Maggie was due—plenty of time, we figured, to get settled. But that little munchkin had other plans and came two weeks early, on July 16.

From the beginning, Sam loved his little sister and would invent games to entertain her. One of his favorites was a game he called "Super Baby." This game involved Maggie sitting in an ExerSaucer while Sam pulled out all manner of tricks to try to get a baby-laugh out of her. She would be all smiles while he made paper hats for each of them and then turned flips and acted out superhero scenes until he got the high-pitched, gleeful giggle he was going for. Sam would spread out his arms as though he were flying around Maggie. He always made her the hero who saved the world—hence "Super Baby."

Sam was in kindergarten when 9/11 happened. I think every adult remembers exactly where she was when those planes flew into the World Trade Center. Maggie was just over a year old, and I was entertaining her in our playroom. The phone rang. It was my friend Gail.

"Nina, turn on your TV," she said.

I went into the family room and, holding Maggie, stood in shock as Gail and I talked about what could possibly be happening. I hung up with Gail and called Jeff. He knew about the crash into the towers, but, unlike me, did not leap to the belief that there might be some residual risk for us. Jeff—always the optimist. All I knew at that moment was that I needed to get Sam home. I wanted to circle the wagons.

I made the five-minute drive to Suwanee Elementary School and checked Sam out. I was not the only parent to do so. In the car, Sam asked why I had gotten him early. I gave him a vague answer about thinking it would be nice to give him a half-day off. Even at five years old, Sam had the capacity to worry when he saw something scary on TV. I saw no reason why he needed to know more at that time. Back at home, he played with his matchbox cars while Maggie napped, and I watched the unfolding horror.

After the attack, the hotel business dropped into a record bust, and my contracts dried up. For years afterward, I was unable to find work that fit all my prerogatives: a contracted hotel job that was part-time and allowed me to tele-commute. I became a full-time stay-at-home mom for a while, and I was not sad about this. I loved being home and available for my children. Our family's finances were stable enough, so there didn't seem to be a downside.

On Mother's Day weekend, 2002, our neighborhood had a community-wide garage sale. It was a semi-annual event for the neighborhood, planned by the Homeowners Association. All you had to do to participate was set up items in your garage and driveway and wait for cars to drive by. The day of the event was sunny and mild, and I planned to sit outside in a folding chair for part of the day and maybe make some extra cash. I thought it would be a good opportunity to get rid of maternity clothes and baby items.

Maggie was almost two, Sam was six, I was 35, and Jeff was 42. We agreed that we had our hands full with two children. I asked Jeff to get a vasectomy, but he said he didn't want to do that until he was 45. When I asked why, he said some guy he knew regretted getting a vasectomy during his first marriage because he later married someone younger who wanted a baby. I was incredulous and responded by asking him if he had someone better waiting in the wings! (Jeff responded by saying of course he didn't have anyone waiting in the wings, and he would get a vasectomy—eventually. The argument ended in a stalemate.)

The week after the garage sale, my period was a little late. My breasts felt a little heavy. I went to Walgreens and bought a pregnancy test. It was positive.

When I told Jeff, he was as shocked as I was. I had been on a low-dose estrogen birth control pill, and it should have worked.

I must have missed a dose. I made an appointment with my gynecologist—Dr. E., who had delivered Maggie—who confirmed the pregnancy. I told him this was unexpected. I was concerned, given my age and the three previous miscarriages, one of which had been due to trisomy, a fetal abnormality incompatible with life. Dr. E. warned me that the chance of a successful pregnancy this time was less than sixty percent. He ordered chorionic villus sampling, a prenatal test for birth defects, genetic diseases, and other problems. Happily, the test found no genetic disorders or birth defects. I was pregnant with a perfectly healthy baby girl.

Soon after the test, Jeff and I made a plan to tell six-year-old Sam about the baby. One night before his bedtime, Jeff asked him to come up to our bedroom. Sam walked into our room, his dinosaur-printed pajamas riding up on his quickly elongating body. I asked him to sit with me on the small settee. I put my arm around his shoulders.

"Sam, we have some news," I said.

"What?! We're finally going to Disney World?!" he asked. He had a neighborhood friend who had just vacationed at this magical place, and he had been pestering us about going ever since.

"We are going to have another baby, and she is a girl."

Sam shook off my arm and abruptly stood up and faced us.

"No! I know you are kidding me. We don't need another baby! We really don't need another girl!"

I wasn't sure if his anger was more about the baby or the missed trip to Disney World. But he was not happy with the news.

Jeff and I worked to reassure him that we had the capacity to love three children equally and to always be there for him. He seemed to absorb what we were saying but didn't seem sure that we were being truthful.

AFTER THE BABY'S arrival, Sam easily adjusted to having Claire in our life. At age seven, he was more concerned with school and sports, and Jeff and I were able to tag team enough so that he didn't miss anything. Maggie, however, had a tougher time accepting the new arrival to our family. When my parents brought Maggie and Sam to visit Claire and me in the hospital, Maggie climbed up on the hospital bed to be next to me. She was not quite two-and-a-half. Pointing to herself, she said, "But, Mommy, I'm the baby. It's me, Maggie."

My heart melted. I said a silent prayer. *God, please help me be able to spread an equal amount of love and care to each of these children. Each is a precious gift that I must guard with my life. Please make me strong enough to do this well.*

As Sam got older, I often described him as the voice of reason in a house full of chaos. Sam was generally above the fray. He could be reasonable and insightful. With his half-smile and dry jokes, he brought all back into perspective. Once when we were at the dinner table, I was trying to get five-year-old Maggie to try a lentil dish I had made. She was stubbornly refusing to taste it and we were at a standoff. Sam, nine at the time, addressed the table and said, "Why did the tomato get embarrassed? Because it saw the chick pee!" We all giggled, and the tenseness of the moment dissipated. Sam had a preternatural ability to see through the shenanigans and into the real heart of the matter.

One thing Sam was *not* laid-back about, however, was competition of any sort. He hated to lose. When he was young, losing a board game could throw him into a tantrum. He was also competitive at school, though in a quieter way. In second grade, he was elected the overall winner in the Accelerated Reader program. He was happy to have won, but he never participated in the program again. He told me it was because he wanted to choose books he was interested in rather than work through a given list of titles in order to earn points. That was probably true, but I also suspected he didn't want to risk not winning the next year.

In early grade school, Sam was accepted into American Mensa after scoring in the 99th percentile on the cognitive abilities tests he took in first grade, third grade, and fifth grade. To qualify for Mensa, one must have scored in the top two percent of the general population on an accepted, standardized intelligence test at any point in one's life. An estimated two percent of Americans are eligible for membership. When we received Sam's letter of acceptance from Mensa, Jeff and I were surprised and proud. At the time, Sam was too young to appreciate the significance of belonging in this society. (Since his death, I occasionally look at Sam's email account, and to this day, he gets mail from American Mensa. I've wondered if his exceptional brain was part of what made it difficult for him to be here.)

Sam was not the only competitive one. I felt that my children's successes or failures were a direct reflection on me. Each quiz bowl contest, test, speech, or sports game literally caused me physical pain, so badly did I want my children to do well. The pain would start as a tightening in my throat and become a tension in my neck that moved to my chest and developed into a tightness between my eyes that blurred my sight. I had never had such a visceral reaction to anything that *I* had striven for, and I was amazed when I first experienced this with my children. Even after the event was over, or the test scores were released, or acceptance letters for college were either issued or not, I couldn't let go, reliving every aspect of the experience, whether it resulted in disappointment or triumph. Despite Sam's fierce independence, I would belatedly strategize how I could have or should have better helped him succeed. I realize now that this is not the best approach to parenting. It's important for children to experience failures and learn to overcome them. But when it comes to a mother's love, reason is not foremost in the mix. I would feel a real heartbreak for every misstep.

I love my three children immensely. As a young adult, I had not really believed you could love and care about the wellbeing of someone else more than you cared for yourself. But I'd never had a child. Now, I absolutely understand the stories of mothers who step in front of a vehicle or into the path of a bullet to save their child's life.

Once, while in high school, Sam said to me, "Mom, you are too invested in me." I denied it. I tried hard to believe that I wasn't overly obsessed with my kids and their futures. Besides my three children, I had a part-time job, hobbies like tennis and running, several friends, a husband, an extended family—an overall well-rounded life. But, to be perfectly honest, I often lay awake at night worrying and hoping that my children would have happy, easy, and successful lives. The emotions and love and belief in them outweighed everything my conscious mind told me. I thought that by fiercely loving my kids, I would protect them. *Would God take away a child who is so cherished?*

CHAPTER 3

Picking Up from Chapter 1

It had been 24 hours since anyone had heard from Sam. During this time, we'd texted and called, but his phone had always gone straight to voicemail. We'd checked his bank account, and there had been no activity. Jeff had called Verizon, but because Sam had turned his phone off, they could not pick up any ping to locate him. We'd contacted every person we could think of who might know his whereabouts. We drove to places we thought he could be. The Gwinnett Police Department, the Suwanee Police Department, and the Georgia Tech Police Department were all looking for him. I was physically and mentally exhausted. Call it mother's intuition, but I knew our situation was perilous. I just knew.

Not long after Hannah's call about the post on Reddit, Jeff called the Gwinnett Police Department and asked for any update. He could not get much information on the search for Sam from the detective on the call, and I was feeling desperate. I called Angela and asked if she knew of a private investigator. Her husband, Greg, was a tax attorney, and I knew he had connections with attorneys and judges in Atlanta. Within thirty minutes, Angela called me back and gave me a name and phone number. I called right away. I told the investigator of our situation, and we scheduled a meeting within the hour at an office in downtown Atlanta. He told me his fee to start an investigation was $2,400. At that point, he could have told me anything; I was not concerned about money.

Jeff grabbed the checkbook, and we rushed to our minivan. As we drove south on the interstate, I reluctantly called Hannah and asked her to meet us at the detective's office. I did not want to see her, but I wanted her there in case there was something, anything that she knew that we didn't. On the call, Hannah reminded me that her parents had taken away her car—I still wasn't clear exactly why. She said she would ask a friend to take her downtown. Her friend would drop her off, and she would ride back home with us. When we arrived at the building where the investigator's office was—a skyscraper downtown—Hannah was already there.

Jeff and I walked into the lobby and saw Hannah having a conversation with the detective. They were sitting in leather chairs pulled close to one another. As we walked up, they fell silent.

The detective led us to a quieter part of the lobby, where the four of us stood. In both looks and manner, the investigator reminded me of the character of Bunk from *The Wire*; a tough, streetwise detective. Before he began asking us questions, he matter-of-factly asked for the $2,400 retainer fee. I handed him the check. After answering his questions, I started to worry that this was a waste of time and money. He was calling all the same police departments that we had earlier. We stood in the lobby, listening to him have "Hey, buddy" conversations with cop friends.

While we were there, Jeff received a call from the Gwinnett Police. He went into an alcove to take the call. Ignoring the detective and Hannah, I stood just feet from Jeff, watching his body language. He was talking quietly so that I could not hear the conversation.

Jeff came back to us. In a flat voice, he said, "The police found Sam." I searched Jeff's expression for any glimmer of hope. Hannah screamed for joy that Sam had been found and hugged me. I didn't hug her back.

"Is he alive?" I asked Jeff.

He said they would not tell him over the phone, but the police would meet us at our home as soon as we could get there. He reached over to where the $2,400 check still lay on a countertop and tore it in half. As we drove home, I felt like something had died inside me. I tried to pray that Sam was alive even if that meant in jail or in a hospital—but if that were the case, why would they want to meet us at home? I had an overwhelming feeling that my prayers were fruitless.

Hannah was chatting to us and saying over and over, "Thank God he is alive."

Jeff solemnly asked her, "Do you feel like Sam's been more depressed lately? Has anything happened to make him feel more depressed?"

She said that Sam had seemed good lately. Her voice was vivacious, and she seemed excited. I suddenly found her presence intolerable. I hated that she seemed to take so much pleasure in being the center of attention, first with the detective, and now with Jeff. I hated that she was so stupid to think that Sam was okay.

She asked Jeff a question, but before he could answer, I snapped, "Could we stop with the banal chitchat? We don't even know if he's alive!" The conversation abruptly stopped.

En route, Hannah's mom texted me and said that Hannah had told her that the police had found Sam. "Thank God," she wrote.

I texted her back. "We don't think he is alive. Please come pick Hannah up from our house."

It was late afternoon by then, and the sun had begun to cut lower in the sky, as it does in those last weeks of wintertime. We rode the remaining miles to our home in silence. But it did not feel silent in my head. I heard every conversation I'd had with Sam over the last weeks play over and over, an unrelenting cacophony of everything I'd said or done wrong.

At home, Maggie was waiting for us in the kitchen. Her arms were wrapped close to her body, holding her small frame tightly. She looked like she had been crying. I hugged her. She told us two police officers had come to our house while she had been there alone. When she'd told them we weren't home yet, the officers had said they would be back later. They had not told her anything.

Within five minutes, a pair of Gwinnett police officers, a woman and a man both in uniform, came to our door and asked whether they could come in. In our family room, the male officer took a seat. The female officer remained standing, just behind her partner. Jeff and I were sitting together on the sofa. Maggie and Hannah were standing. I felt my heartbeat throbbing in my ears and felt my nails cutting crescents into my palms. Life seemed strangely still. In the breath before the male deputy started speaking, I fleetingly wondered if I could cause a distraction to keep him from opening his mouth. I didn't.

"I'm sorry to inform you both, but your son is deceased."

Before he finished the sentence, I began to scream into Jeff's neck. I wanted to drown the officer out. Holding onto me, Jeff asked about the cause of death, and the officer said that the coroner would be in touch with that information. I continued to scream, willing my shouts to unmake the truth.

In between sobs, I asked to be taken to Sam. I insisted that I see his body now, or I would never believe them. I wanted to prove them wrong. Jeff quietly counseled me that this would not be a good idea. The officers said it was impossible because he was already with the coroner. My body folded into Jeff's. All I wanted was for my body and mind to give out and die. This could not be true.

When I did look up, Hannah was still standing in shocked silence. I scarcely regarded her and turned my eyes on my Maggie. She was standing near Hannah. I walked over to her and wrapped her in my arms. As I held her, she asked, "Mom, what will we do?"

I led her to the sofa, and we sat together in numb disbelief. Vaguely, I took notice of the events unfolding around us. The deputies left. Hannah's mother came to collect her. She spoke with Jeff, but I did not talk to her. Our next-door neighbor cornered Hannah and her mom as they left our house to find out what was going on. Almost immediately, neighbors showed up and asked what they could do.

The state of shock must be some type of protection for the body and the mind. I felt suspended in time, unable to comprehend what was going on around me. I didn't truly believe anything was real.

How was I just sitting there? How was I answering when asked questions? This sense of shock was to become my new normal in the weeks to come.

Anticipating Claire's bus at 4:30, Maggie and I waited for her by the front door, looking at her through the sidelights. I watched her outside talking with her friend and noticed when she caught a glimpse of our faces—later, she said she'd known the news about Sam would be bad. She'd dawdled because she had not wanted to hear the truth, and in that moment, I envied her lack of knowledge about Sam's death. I wanted to go back to the unbelieving, too.

Claire walked into the foyer and let her backpack slide from her shoulders. Without much preamble, I told her that Sam was gone. Tears sprung into her eyes, and I held her tight. It would be the first of many tellings of Sam's loss we would have to do.

My parents and my sister Amanda arrived soon after Claire. I had texted them that morning to let them know that Sam was missing, and the three of them had immediately set out on the six-hour drive from west Tennessee to our house. I met them at the front door and looked at their expectant faces. Feeling I could not bear the hope they still showed, while they were still on our front steps, I blurted out, "He's dead. Sam has died." They rushed to hold me.

Our family, now of four, along with my parents and sister, sat in the family room in collective shock. No one spoke. My dad sat stoically while my mom wept without making noise. Maggie and Claire sat together on the floor, almost touching. My sister took on the role of caretaker and asked the girls if she could get them anything, do anything for them. They both politely said they were okay. At some point, Jeff walked into the kitchen and called the coroner. He spoke quietly on the phone. The conversation was short.

I waited for him to end the call before I walked the few steps into the kitchen. He was leaning against the island with his head in his hands. I touched his sleeve and asked the question I was both desperate and afraid to know. "How?"

"He hanged himself."

I could not comprehend this. Why would he kill himself in such a violent way? I started sobbing in big gulps and leaned against Jeff. He kept an arm around me, but his own body seemed to sag and deflate. When I looked up, Claire was standing in the doorway to the kitchen, silent.

My sister came to me and urged me to go lie down. Instead of going to my bedroom, I went downstairs to the basement, to Sam's room. I lay on his unmade bed, inhaling the scent of him and wailing in a voice that must not have sounded human.

CHAPTER 4

The Aftermath

Throughout that weekend, friends and family came to the house and offered support. I have little memory of who was there and what was said. Somehow Friday night and Saturday passed. Jeff was there greeting people, thanking them, and attending to details. I was grateful that he took charge; I felt physically incapable of doing anything. I mostly sat in one corner of our sofa and was unable to move.

Good friends showed up. Our neighbor Connie made a call to our pastor to let him know we wanted him to lead the service. It was a relief to not make the call myself—I didn't yet have the words to tell of our tragedy. One friend put together a slideshow of pictures of Sam for the service and arranged for her husband and daughter to play a violin duet during the service. Other friends organized a reception to be held at our house after the funeral. Neighbors and friends generously helped with the food. Yet another friend used her photography skills to create a beautifully framed portrait of Sam. Meals were brought and would continue to be delivered to us for weeks.

There were so many kindnesses done for us that I do not remember them all. I hesitate to cite any names, because I would, of course, leave someone out. But even in the fog of my grief, I was amazed by the love shown to us.

SATURDAY MORNING, JEFF and I went to the funeral home and met with the director and our pastor to finalize the details. There were many things to decide. Which songs would be sung, which people would speak, which urn would hold his ashes. The only thing I remember explicitly saying was that because Sam had taken his life, I did not want anyone saying or indicating that his place in Heaven was in doubt. I had been told in childhood that those who commit suicide do not go to Heaven. Pastor Dave relieved me by replying with a gentle smile and saying, "Of course not, no Christian churches still believe that."

That evening, the funeral home called Jeff. Sam's body was prepared, and they wanted to know whether we wished to see him. Feeling shaky, I rose from the couch and began to put my shoes on. I felt an urgent need to see Sam, as though viewing his body might give me any answers or comfort. I looked at my parents apologetically. I told them I thought Jeff and I should go alone. They nodded their agreement.

At the funeral home, we were ushered into the room where my beautiful boy lay in a coffin. I touched Sam's face. His skin was shockingly cold—ice cold. I jerked my hand away. "Get him a blanket," I said to Jeff. He told me, as gently as such a detail can be delivered, that Sam had been in a refrigeration unit. I stared wildly at Jeff and shook my head no, over and over. One more horrifying image to add to my tormented psyche—the thought of my baby on a steel shelf in a giant refrigerator.

My most handsome son looked just like himself. He was wearing the shirt, tie, and blazer that my sister and I had chosen for him to wear. He looked like he was asleep. I touched his hair. It felt coarser than usual, but, as Sam would have wanted, well-coiffed. I kissed his high cheekbone. I tried to hold his hand but stopped at once. It was cold and lifeless and hard, like that of a mannequin. I had the overwhelming desire to grab Sam's shoulder, to pull him out of the coffin and hold him and attempt to breathe life back into him. I have no idea how Jeff got me out of the room. He drove me home, where I took medication and fell into a fretful, horrid sleep.

Somehow, I managed to attend church the next day. Looking back, I cannot imagine why I felt I needed to do this. Or, in fact, *how*

I did. Joining us at church were my mom, my dad, and my brother Rusty and my sister-in-law Lisa, who had arrived Saturday night. My sister, Amanda, stayed behind to clean and prepare the house for the frequent visitors and upcoming reception. After the service, all eight of us, including Maggie and Claire, filed into the pastor's office. I can't remember much of what was discussed. I suppose some last-minute details about the funeral.

After church, we returned home, and I went upstairs and got into my bed. I stayed there until late in the afternoon. When I came downstairs, Jeff told me he had started on an obituary. He asked me to make edits. The fact that I was able to do that or anything else attests to how the body protects itself through the mechanism of shock.

Samuel "Sam" Jeffrey Owen, age 20, passed away on February 26, 2016. His passing was sudden and unexpected.

Sam was a kind-hearted, sensitive individual who was compassionate toward all people in all of life's circumstances. Sam was an excellent student who made straight A's throughout high school and near-perfect scores on standardized tests. Sam graduated North Gwinnett High School in 2014 with honors and was currently a sophomore at the Georgia Institute of Technology, studying Physics.

Sam was a tremendous brother and son to his sisters and parents. He was always willing to help in any way needed, by anyone who asked. Besides tutoring and charitable works, he was selfless in everyday acts of generosity, both in word and in deed.

Sam is survived by his loving family and many friends. The loss of this beautiful mind and near-perfect heart will never be reconciled in the minds of his family. We are less without him. Our only solace is that he is in a better place where he is already affecting others. The family asks that in lieu of flowers, please send any memorial donations to the animal shelter or the mental health charity of your choice.

CHAPTER 5

An Impossible Goodbye

Monday evening, Jeff and I arrived at the funeral home before the set time for the visitation service to begin. I remember fleetingly wondering why funeral homes are always cold (To postpone the decomposition of the bodies lying in repose?) and whether all funeral homes smelled the same. (Musty, heavily scented with roses, mums, and lilies, and something else, something chemical.) I had been to a viewing or wake only a handful of times in my life. A memory of being in a funeral home where my grandmother lay in a coffin had stayed with me. I had been sixteen at the time, and I recall being uneasy about the ritual of the viewing. I was confused that people were laughing and talking about trivial things in the same room as my grandmother's corpse. Even now, I'm struck by the odd rituals our culture goes through when grieving a death.

I don't remember ever being asked whether we should have Sam's casket open or closed. He looked beautiful, impeccable in the shirt, tie, and jacket my sister had helped me choose. Closing the coffin on him was impossible for me. I knew he no longer inhabited that body, but, just for now, I wanted to still see him and touch him.

Just before the visitation time was to begin, Hannah came into the room. She walked up to Sam's coffin, made a wild, animal-like scream, and collapsed onto the floor. I didn't address Hannah but remember asking someone to get her out of the room. I could hardly keep my anger at her in check. I wanted to rage at her—perhaps so that I wouldn't have to rage at myself or Sam.

Within minutes of Hannah being led out, a long line of friends and family began to file into the room. There were over 300 visitors there. Jeff stayed at the entrance to greet people, and I stood beside Sam's casket. I wanted Jeff to stand with me. I felt that he needed to be beside me to support me both psychologically and physically, if needed. But because of the throng of visitors, I couldn't get word to him.

There were many hugs and tears. Sam's friends approached me, some by themselves, some with their parents. Although all hugged me, many could scarcely make prolonged eye contact. I knew it must be hard for them to face the death of a friend, a person as young as they were. His friends stood uncomfortably in front of me, shifting their weight from one foot to the other. The tears of disbelief in their eyes matched how I felt. They told me how much Sam was loved and respected. They relayed to me how central he was in their lives. I felt appreciation toward them, for the willingness of these young men and women to show such vulnerability.

Work colleagues of mine and Jeff's came for the viewing, some from out of state. My boss, Lisa, had spoken to one of my other colleagues and remarked what a senseless tradition it is to have a heartbroken mother stand beside her child's coffin and greet mourners.

I stood to greet most of the visitors, but at some point, someone brought up a chair for me to sit in. People were kind. We made it through the two hours.

The next day, we would have Sam's funeral. For that, his coffin would be closed.

Before leaving the funeral home, I stood facing Sam. I touched his arm and kissed his cheek. For the last time, I looked at the beautiful fringe of eyelashes closed on his cheeks, seeing not just him in this moment, but him as he had come into the world. For the last time, I looked at the mole on the left side of his chin. For the last time, I looked at his handsome face and trim physique. For the last time, I looked at my first-born, my son.

From My Journal

Tuesday, March 1, 2016

My darling boy,

Today was your funeral. The turnout was tremendous. The tears of your friends, my friends, Dad's friends, and our family were endless and heart-wrenching. Your coffin sat closed at the front of the room with beautiful flowers laid on top. I could not even guess how many people were at the church. As we walked down the aisle to a pew in front, I held Claire's hand, and Dad held Maggie's. I was holding myself together by the most tenuous of strings and did not look around at the other mourners.

Pastor Dave gave the eulogy, and he did a remarkable job. One line that would have made you smile was, "How many of you felt good about your SAT scores or your GPA until you heard about Sam's scores and grades?" The somber crowd smiled. Then he continued, "But Sam did not make people feel dumb because he had a heart filled with kindness and compassion so that he treated all people and all living things gently. All things gently, except for himself."

Dave went on to talk about your generous nature and how you were never too busy to help anyone else out. Four others spoke as well, our neighbor Greg, your uncle David, Dhroov, and Hannah.

Greg talked about the first time he met you and the example you set as a big brother to his kids and ours. He spoke of your sweet effusive smile evident in a picture they have of you on their refrigerator. To close his speech, Greg read this poem:

Do not judge a biography by its length
Nor by the number of pages in it
Judge it by the richness of its contents
Sometimes those unfinished are among the most poignant

Do not judge a song by its duration
Nor by the number of its notes
Judge it by the way it touches and lifts the soul
Sometimes those unfinished are among the most beautiful
And when something has enriched your life
And when its melody lingers on in your heart
Is it unfinished?
Or is it endless?

—Author Unknown

Your Uncle David spoke next, and he talked about what a sweet, intelligent nephew you were. How soft-spoken you were, but how everything you said was worth hearing. He spoke about your values—the value you held for all animals and people. He said he was proud to be your uncle.

Your friend Dhroov was the third person to speak. He spoke about your mutual love of music and how much you opened his eyes to other types of music. He, Nabeel, and Ibrahim are having such a hard time dealing with your death.

Lastly, Hannah went to the podium. I did not want her to speak and had told your dad, but he—without my knowledge—allowed it to happen. I was afraid she would be a total mess and once again, as she had done at the funeral home, make it the "Hannah Show."

Surprisingly, she was eloquent and poignant. She spoke of her love for you. She mentioned how she was with you when you got your tattoo and told the story of how well that went over with me! And, she also said how hurt she was that you left without a goodbye.

I have to say that leaving without a goodbye, stings me too. The morning you died, I gave you the idea about accompanying me to Dallas, and you acted like it was a passable idea. Did you know then? Why? Why that day? Was there a trigger? Is it my fault?

IN PREPARATION FOR the visitation and funeral, my friend Robin had set up notecards and pens for anyone who wanted to write a memory of Sam. She placed a basket nearby for them to deposit these memories. Several people wrote notes, which we later read. Besides these, we also have memories of Sam written by friends on Reddit and other social media. Jeff combined these in a document and then printed it out. I have probably read through this document fifty times. Having a glimpse into how his peers saw him is precious to me. What follows is just a portion of the posts and notes:

You were one of my closest friends Sam. My freshman year of college primarily consists of you, me, and our other close friends, just chilling in your room listening to dope music. You exposed me to the world of hip-hop and culture that I've never seen before. The music you showed me—I still listen to it all the time. Your views on the world were unique, you were a true philosopher. The experiences we shared: eye-opening, the stuff we've done, the risks we took, I look back and laugh, we were such fools! But it was in good fun. Without you Sam, my freshman year would have been dull, and sad, you made me defy the typical Georgia Tech student stereotype. I would have been no different. You would have been a great physicist man, you had the intelligence, no doubt, but you also had the natural curiosity that great scientists have. Your personality, your wit, your charm—it lives on in all of us, man. I never really liked trap music that much Sam, you knew that, but today, I played Gucci Mane, one last time.

I only first met Sam during the beginning of our freshman year, but since then it's felt like forever. I'd always admired his sense of style; he was definitely the coolest member of our group. Sam was always a relaxed and agreeable kind of guy, never quick to anger. Our group circled around him; he felt like a natural leader. Without him, our crew will always be one member short.

It is such a tragedy for our community and nation to lose such a talented and warm soul at this young age.

I met Sam when I fell asleep on his shoulder on the long flight to France a couple of summers ago. He was such a sweet guy and incredibly smart. I wish he realized just how special he truly was. So, so special.

I learned of Sam's passing from a friend who is a co-worker of Mr. Owen. I remember Sam as his first name because it is the same as my son's. Sam came into the running store where I work right before the Gwinnett County High School county finals his senior year. He had questions about nutrition before his meet, as he told me that he was trying to swim a state qualifying time. We had a wonderful conversation, and I remember being quite impressed and taken with what a mature, intelligent, and composed young man he was. I asked him what events he was swimming, and I told him that I would be cheering for him as I would be attending the meet watching my daughter swim. I remember watching his reaction as he swam his qualifying time, and I was so happy for him when he met his goal.

Sam Owen was one of the most intelligent young men I have ever had the pleasure to meet. His intentions were not always understood, but his mind was full of knowledge and his heart full of love for all.

People make decisions we don't understand every day, but I know in my soul that Sam Owen would never make an illogical decision if he thought there was another way.

Sam may be gone, but the knowledge and respect he taught me will never die while I, and those I influence, walk the earth. I love you, God loves you, and the memory of Sam Owen will always live on.

Dear Owen Family,

I wanted to share with you how your son changed my life without ever knowing it.

In high school, I suffered from severe depression and reached a point in my sophomore year where I felt broken and alone. I spent all my time between school, work, and church and felt like I had very few, if any, close friends. Junior year I decided I needed to take some initiative and branch out to new people. Sam was one of those people. We sat together with a pretty large group of people at lunch every day. Sam was always welcoming and kind, even though others were not. He made me laugh all the time and made me feel like I belonged. I owe him my life for that.

I've known Sam since about second grade. I still remember the first time I met him. Our moms had a tennis match, so I went over to his house because my parents weren't home. He was playing video games, and I sat down to join. We've been friends ever since. I remember swimming with him every summer. I remember his birthday parties. I remember that time we camped out in his backyard. I have so many wonderful memories with Sam. I will never forget these memories, and I will cherish them forever.

I never met Sam, but my son, Alex, considered him a friend and spoke of him often. He talked about how brilliant he was, and how happy Sam was to help with his papers—editing and ideas for content. They had several classes together, and Sam was the one who Alex respected the most. I know they had deep conversations—and their friendship was deeper than just a surface relationship—even though they didn't hang out outside of class.

Sam was one of the most genuinely kind, smart, and funny people that I have ever had the pleasure to meet. I will never forget Spring Break in Panama City our senior year of high school. There was never a moment with Sam that I wasn't smiling or laughing. He was always supportive with swimming, school, and life in general. Sam was a one-of-a-kind friend, and he will always live on in our memories.

PART II

SAM'S DECLINE

*"The world is indeed full of peril, and in it there are many dark places;
but still there is much that is fair, and though in all lands love is now
mingled with grief, it grows perhaps the greater."*

—J.R.R. TOLKIEN, *The Fellowship of the Ring*

CHAPTER 6

Searching for Answers

Just days after Sam's death, it became important to me to reconstruct the last hours of his life. Perhaps this seems unnecessary and strange. But I had to know what had changed from how he had seemed the night before and the morning of his death. We had had conversations. He had seemed fine. Was there a text, email, phone call, or in-person conversation that had made February 25 the day he would no longer walk on this Earth?

During this amateur forensics investigation, Jeff and I tried to put together a timeline of the days, hours, and moments that had led to Sam's death. We pored over his computer, his phone, and anything else we could find. We spoke with anyone who might have seen him in those last days.

We will never have all the answers, but we can somewhat trace his actions over his last few days.

In the weeks and months after Sam's death, we would also uncover text messages, handwritten journals, and Google documents filled with his own writing about his activities and mental state, along with papers and essays he'd written for school assignments; some of those writings, I will share here. In reading the documents, I began to feel that Sam had been impulsive in taking his own life. Life seemed to be going better for him the days before he died. I share his writings here in part because I believe that working to understand impulsive suicide attempts is necessary for effective interventions for others. One study by the NIH showed that 48 percent of attempters were impelled by sudden inclinations to attempt suicide.[1]

---

1. https://www.ncbi.nlm.nih.gov/pmc/articles/PMC4965648/.

ON MONDAY, FEBRUARY 22, Sam was home doing homework. Claire put out a group text to our family sharing that she had run 2.5 miles that day in PE. Sam's response:

He and Claire then talked about "lefty struggles," such as getting inky fingers when writing. (They were both left-handed, whereas the rest of us were right-handed.) That evening at 6:30, Sam had an appointment with Brad, a life coach and hypnotherapist. Sam had started seeing Brad at the beginning of January for hypnotherapy, and this would be his third session with him. The sessions focused on helping Sam increase his self-esteem and motivation for school.

Hannah texted Sam, wanting to go with him. She said she would sit in the car during his session. Sam never answered her texts. His phone shows that she had called him five times that day between 1:20 p.m. and 3:30 p.m. and texted him nine times. Sam went to his session alone.

On Tuesday and Wednesday, February 23 and 24, Sam went to class at Georgia Tech. He took notes, including marking down information about an exam that would be upcoming that Monday. At the bottom of his notes, he had doodled a funny little alien figure.

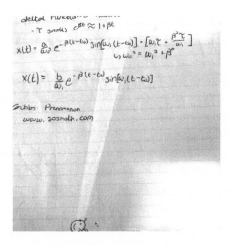

That Wednesday evening at 5:00, Sam went with Jeff to a local barbecue restaurant to pick up dinner for the family. Sam was group texting us and telling Maggie that they forgot her mac-n-cheese. He teasingly told her minutes later that he had secured it and that she should call him "Com Truise." He chatted easily with us while we ate the meal at home. We discussed Hillary versus Bernie for the Democratic nomination. I was an ardent supporter of Hillary, whereas Sam thought Bernie had all the answers.

Around 6:30 p.m., Sam came to me and said that Hannah had phoned and was telling him that her parents had kicked her out of the house and that she had nowhere else to go. Having been burned by her lies before, he asked if I would text her mom to ask whether that were true.

I sent the following message: "Hi, it's Nina, Sam's mom. Your daughter has told Sam that she has been kicked out of her house and has nowhere to go. We care about Hannah, but with two young daughters, I am not equipped to have her stay with us. Is it true? Have you asked her to leave?"

Hannah's mother texted back, "No, it is not true. We took her car from her. Did something happen between our kids?"

I replied, "Sam just said she started giving him ultimatums about staying with her or she'd hurt herself. She didn't want him going home last week to finish homework, and he feels very torn and responsible for her. But he isn't healthy enough himself to be accountable for anyone else."

Hannah's mom texted back, "I was worried that something like that was happening. It's part of her illness and she has lost more than one important relationship."

I relayed the text conversation to Sam, telling him that Hannah had not been kicked out of her parents' home. He shook his head sadly and said, "That's what I thought."

Later that evening, Sam went to work for a couple of hours, delivering pizza. He was home by 10:00 p.m., and sometime after, in a red spiral notebook, he created a pros-and-cons list about staying with or breaking up with Hannah. (After Sam's death, Jeff and I met with his psychologist; he told us that he had recommended Sam do this to sort out his feelings.) The pros column began:

- We tend to have a lot of fun together.
- We enjoy similar things.
- Great sexual chemistry.

He cited a magazine interview he had read that advised men should marry someone "who loves you more than you do them." Under a bullet point that said "she loves me a lot," he had underlined "a lot." He also wrote that being with Hannah had improved his self-esteem. When I read this, I felt remorse for anything I had said to encourage the breakup.

Heartbreakingly, the last item on his pros list was, "all this makes me so sad."

In the cons column, Sam began by focusing on surface subjects, such as:

- I don't feel the same level of affection or attraction toward her as she does towards me.
- I don't really care for many of her tastes.
- Can't help but feel that I'm settling.

He also noted concerns about his and her mental health. He wrote, "We are both in recovery and maybe shouldn't be in a relationship." He said that Hannah "seems to have issues with social boundaries" and that "she's deceptive and needy and seems to bring out [my] less desirable habits, e.g., smoking."

Reading this later, I couldn't help but be impacted by Sam's logic and his concern for his own recovery. *How did all of that change in just a few hours?*

The list ends with hopeful bullet points about his future without Hannah.

- I could benefit from having a partner who better compensates for my weaknesses.
- I've already started to embrace the idea of being single again.

In the margin on the cons side of the page, Sam had written: "Mom is starkly against it."

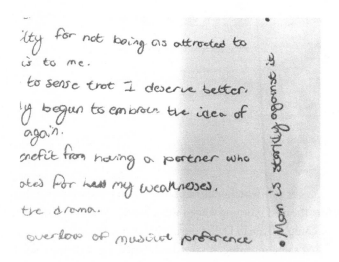

I assume "it" was a continued relationship with Hannah. Reading this after Sam's death, I wished he had not referenced me on this list.

The statement immersed me in guilt. *Why was I so forceful in stating my opinions?* And, harder yet to think, *Was my opinion a factor in his decision to end his life?*

After he completed his pros-and-cons list about breaking up with Hannah, he did some Internet searching: general searches about physics, video games, and then queries about how to break up with a girlfriend.

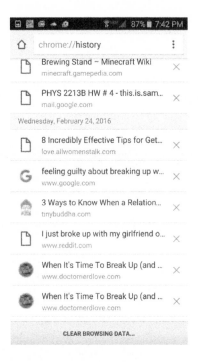

I'm not sure whether he slept that night; I just know that he was asleep the next morning when I woke him to ask whether he wanted to accompany me to Dallas during his spring break.

That same morning, on the day he died, his web searches took a darker turn. He was searching for ways to put his impulsive plan into action. The time stamp on these show that they began at 10:00 a.m. and lasted until 1:30 p.m.

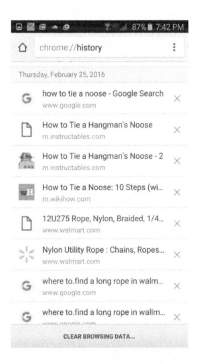

From a receipt found in Sam's car, we know that after leaving our house, he went to the nearby Wal-Mart, where he purchased a Frappuccino, a rope, and a pair of scissors. We do not know whether he drove around afterward, thinking of his intended action, or went straight to downtown Suwanee. There was no activity on his phone.

At some point, he went to a deserted parking lot off Main Street, leaving his Mazda there and walking about a mile along the railroad tracks toward McGinnis Ferry Road. He had left his phone behind in his car, turned off.

From there, Sam went into a wooded area, chose a tree, constructed a noose, climbed that tree, and hanged himself.

THE NEXT DAY, Friday the 26th, the Suwanee Police Department's search party found Sam's body around 1:15 p.m. A little over two hours later, a police officer turned on Sam's phone, and all the unread texts and voicemails from the last twenty-four hours started to light up the screen.

Sam had gone through the effort of taking the passcode off his phone, but, after exploring it carefully, we could not find a suicide note. We never found a note—not on his computer, in his room, on his phone, in his car, in Google docs. Nothing.

The coroner's report read:

> *The decedent was wearing a gray sweatshirt, white t-shirt, denim jeans with a brown belt in the loops of the pants, blue jacket, underwear, black socks, white gym shoes. A pair of scissors, book of matches, and $33 in cash were found in the jacket pocket. A note was not located on nor near the decedent. The investigator pronounced the decedent dead on Friday, February 26, 2016 at 13:45 hours.*

CHAPTER 7

Sam's Writing

Copied from High School AP Psychology Paper, 2013

*M*y mother's pregnancy with me was very much by the books.
Extensive care was put into the avoidance of teratogens, including
the complete abstention from alcohol. To facilitate my in-utero cognitive
development, my mother listened to classical music and read books daily.
Due to a previous miscarriage, she avoided physical activity, despite
working full time, and took the hormone progesterone to prevent a similar happening.

My parents claim that I proceeded relatively quickly through early
language development, surpassing the vast majority of my peers. I learned
new words rapidly and could recite phrases given to me by my parents
at an early age, leading to more human tricks for them to show their
friends. Like all children, I also over-applied grammatical rules and
made up words. I was fortunate to not suffer any impediments to my
acquirement of speech.

For most of my early childhood, I was closest to my mother. This is
mainly because my mother quit working upon my birth while my father
continued to do so full time; therefore, I spent much more time with my
mother and became close to her. Even now, I still feel more emotionally
tied to my mother than my father, although I would consider myself to
be very close to both.

My parents claim that, as a child, I was reasonably easy-going. I
was easy to please and would respond stoically to discipline. I did have
difficulty sleeping through the night, but that was primarily a result of
a lack of scheduling on the part of my parents. Now, I am generally not
emotionally reactive although there have been some strong exceptions to

this tendency. Instead, I tend to internalize strong emotion, especially in a public setting. However, when experiencing severe anger, I may express it physically and have, on occasion, broken things and put holes in walls, and my parents tell me that, even as a young child, I would throw objects when angry. Despite occasional lapses, I am generally calm and patient.

I began thinking abstractly at an early age. At around age nine, I started questioning the existence of God (after being raised Protestant) and the derivation of authority when I should have been only able to think in concrete terms.

For most of my life, I have been a strong advocate of independent thought and the development of individual beliefs and opinions. I associate the emergence of this ideal with my acknowledgment of my atheism. Like most early atheists, I held organized religion in contempt for its proliferation of dogma, and although my antipathy has subsided with maturity, I still firmly hold to the opinion that the autocratic nature of religions that proselytize to convert the sinners, such as Christianity and Islam, is a disservice to free thought.

When a child is told from birth to follow a set of established beliefs under the threat of eternal damnation, there is little room for independent thought. In my view, sheepish subscription to an archaic theology is a travesty, and the clergy, who perpetuate these constrictions to intellectual growth, is the most significant inhibitor to the progress of societal knowledge. Historically, it has been the Religious in the vanguard of the opposition to scientific progress, such as in the cases of Heliocentrism, Evolution, and countless medicinal developments.

I have no aversion to religion nor the religious, but beliefs—metaphysical, ethical, political, etc.—should not be forced onto others. An authority based on dogma without inquiry is not worth following, for, without independent thought and questioning, society stagnates.

To say that adolescence is a difficult time would earn the speaker an award for understatement. The dynamics of sexual maturation, shifting social interactions, and rapidly morphing schemas result in a crucible of psychosocial development, and through this tribulation, according to psychologist Erik Erikson, one develops a personal identity. Following the onset of puberty, I underwent an inane number of ideological shifts: I delved into philosophy, experimented with vegetarianism, and shifted political ideology more times than I care to count, all in search of a true identity. During middle school, I utterly lacked confidence and felt victimized by a culture that failed to understand me; hence, I was scarcely sociable and disallowed myself from enjoying the company of others. As a result, I became anxious about any kind of social interaction or attention directed towards me.

This internal struggle to find a sense of self culminated in a nihilistic crisis that began during my freshman year of high school. I saw little point in putting effort into academics or extracurriculars, and, as is inherent in adolescent egocentrism, I sought no consolation from others. In fact, I became even more misanthropic; I assumed any kindness shown towards me was a deprecating joke or a Tartuffe-esque facade. Fortunately, my condition began to improve at some point during my sophomore year, but the social anxiety and awkwardness remained, and I still had difficulty associating with most people and never formed a solid group of friends.

It is often difficult for teenagers to acknowledge that they are not invincible and that bad things can happen to them. This falsely perceived invincibility is referred to as a personal fable, and it is the cause of adolescents' notorious lack of foresight and caution. During my sophomore year, a certain person—whom I will refer to as "That Kid"—was nominated for homecoming court, as a joke (by somebody else). That year, to cast a ballot in the homecoming elections, all one needed was a student number and an Internet connection, and, just before this development, I had uncovered a roster file, embedded in plain text, containing well over a hundred student IDs. If That Kid were to become the sophomore homecoming king, the resultant hilarity and confusion from the student body would be legendary.

Also, I believed that it would make an appropriate mockery of the archaic popularity contest that is homecoming elections and its associations with cliquishness and social superficiality. Being an adolescent caught up in the moment, I did not think that anything bad would come of me using the roster to give That Kid a bit of an advantage in the elections.

I failed to consider that once somebody casts a vote, they are unable to change it later, so all the people for whom I had helped make a decision realized that they were unable to vote and, eventually, the anomaly was traced back to me. Considering the severity of the offense (over 70 counts of Internet fraudulence, a federal crime, and international crime), I was fortunate to receive a mere four days of suspension and thirty without network privileges. Still, it was enough for me to learn my lesson, and I have not attempted something similarly stupid since.

As I see it, I will remain at my physical peak for a few more years, but then I will begin a slow deterioration that lasts until my eventual expiration. At around age 30, my body will start to weaken, and I will begin to lose some fluid intelligence. At around age 70, I will become increasingly prone to dementia and Alzheimer's disease, which is present in my father's lineage. With that said, aging does not seem like a pleasant process; however, I have come to accept its inevitability. Also, it is reported that older people do not necessarily lose happiness because of age. I presume that this is because aging is a gradual change, and one accommodates these changes into their life over time. My primary concern is that I have already wasted a great deal of the very limited time I have at my peak of learning ability and physical health. I aspire to make the most of my age-related vigor before it is too late.

If there was ever a turning point in my life, it was at the beginning of senior year in high school, when I stopped stressing over what I believed others to think of me. Following this shift in my mantra, I began to gain a reasonable level of confidence and began to speak my mind more often. However, I immediately ran into other barriers, especially the cliquishness that dominates who interacts with whom in high school. As a social floater, I have never strongly associated with a single group and regard such categorization with disdain. Although not belonging to a group makes socializing much more difficult, it has also allowed me to avoid conformity, allowing me to live life for myself and to find an identity that accommodates my set of beliefs, thus preparing myself for adulthood.

It is common for some people to have gregarious social lives in high school but fail to make anything of themselves following graduation. This *is because at adulthood, relationships gain meaning, and without an identity, there is little success in forming intimacy. Because I have been able to establish an identity, I expect that my interactions with others will significantly improve once the focus shifts from social status to quality of personality. In college, I will be much more likely to find people with whom I can identify, due to the high median intellect of the universities to which I am applying and the heightened willingness of people to reach outside of their social comfort zone.*

CHAPTER 8

High School Years

Swimming and video games were both a big part of Sam's adolescent life. The swimming I loved. The gaming, not so much.

Sam started swimming lessons at age three. As a child, I'd learned the basic strokes, but I had never been a strong swimmer. I wanted my kids to learn to swim as an important life skill. Sam began lessons with an instructor named Tanya who taught Infant Swimming Resource. The premise of the method is that if a child accidentally falls into a pool, he or she will know how to flip onto his or her back and float until help arrives. Maggie also started swimming via this method, but at only twelve months old. Six months after the ISR lessons, Sam began private lessons with another instructor. He easily learned strokes and seemed happy in the water. Once, when he was four, he was taking a private lesson at one end of an indoor pool while I sat in a lawn chair on the opposite side. I looked over to see him with his instructor in twelve-foot-deep water, bobbing up and down without any flotation device. After the lesson, I asked her if he was safe doing this. She reassured me by saying, "This kid is completely at ease in water."

Sam began competing in our local summer swim league when he was in first grade. Through the years, he tried other things—soccer, tennis, football—but swimming was the best fit. He had a swimmer's physique, with a long, lean body and long arms. He continued to swim competitively until he graduated high school.

Sam's passion for video games began when he was still in elementary school. At first, there was Game Boy and cartoon-like games.

Later, there would be PC-driven games, GameCube, Wii, and Xbox 360. While Jeff was mildly resistant to purchasing the expensive consoles and games, I wanted Sam to be happy. I indulged my girls similarly with umpteen American Girl dolls and accessories. Perhaps being an indulgent parent makes me weak. But who wants their kid to be sad on Christmas morning?

I limited Sam's screen time, but as he got older, such limits became tougher to enforce. Because his grades were always close to perfect, the argument that he should spend more time studying fell on deaf ears. He was also getting regular, often daily, exercise by swimming.

The aspect I hated most about gaming was how it isolated Sam when I felt he should be spending time with friends and doing things outside. When I would say something in this vein to him, he would always counter that, generally, when friends came over, they wanted to play video games, too.

There is some science out there in favor of gaming, saying that kids who play video games develop problem-solving skills and handle stress better. I'm not sure about the stress part, since I witnessed Sam, more than once, throwing a joystick in frustration after not beating a game. By the time he entered high school, we made a bargain that if gaming was in balance with school, exercise, and extracurriculars, we would allow it. Sam was always obedient and never complained about doing chores around the house, like helping clear the dinner table and taking out the trash. We made our peace with the gaming.

PHYSICALLY, SAM WAS almost preternaturally healthy. He would have an occasional cold or a rare case of strep, but that was the worst of it. He never broke a bone. He never had any surgery, stitches, or even an emergency room visit. He was never diagnosed with OCD, ADHD, Asperger's Syndrome, or any other "disorder," and he was never put on any medication until he took Accutane at age fourteen.

His freshman year of high school, Sam came to me and said he was concerned about his skin. His face had had a few break-outs, but, being a swimmer, he did not want his back covered with pimples—"backne." Our dermatologist prescribed Accutane. Sam did the necessary bloodwork and the brief mood/thought tests for the few months he was on the medication. He would always tell the doctor that his psyche was fine and answer each question in the most positive way available. "How is your mental well-being on a scale of one to ten, with ten being the best?" Sam would respond with "Ten."

Jeff had reservations about putting Sam on Accutane because of its documented side effects, both physiological and psychological. I was also concerned, but other studies had shown it was safe. Ultimately, I was the one who made the decision to have him go on the medication. After using Accutane for five months, Sam discontinued it. The doctor wanted to keep him on it a little longer, but by this point, Sam's skin looked clear and healthy and he had gotten the needed boost for his self-confidence.

In middle school, Sam had adopted the fashion of brushing his longish hair forward to his eyebrows and then sweeping it off to the side, as well as wearing saggy jeans that showed off the top of his boxer shorts. It was not the most respectable way to dress, I thought, but I believed he had the right to decide how he presented himself. And most of his peers were rocking the same look. *Choose your battles,* I thought.

The summer before starting high school, Sam chose a haircut that was cropped close in the back and over his ears but left a little longer and brushed back in the front. I thought it made him look handsome and just a bit more grown-up. (Sam's thick hair was always a bit of a genetic mystery. Neither Jeff nor I have thick hair, and the texture of both of ours is fine, not coarse like Sam's.) He also started dressing better—dark, tailored jeans or chinos, button-down shirts with the sleeves rolled to his elbows, and stylish tennis shoes. I have always enjoyed and cared about clothes, and Sam seemed to have followed suit. I liked that he felt the same way about keeping up good appearances. It felt like another way that he and I were alike.

During his freshman and sophomore years, I believed Sam was doing well in all aspects of his life and rarely worried that he would take any unnecessary risks. He was by no means a perfect kid; no such child exists. He was occasionally moody, but no more than other teens his age. But parents know only what we know. The truth is often withheld from us by our children. I wish I had known of the thoughts and feelings he expressed in the previous chapter. There is such honest insight written there that I like to think it would have helped me to better understand him.

As far as I could discern, Sam's personality had two major facets: he was competitive to the point of being endlessly self-driven, and he was generally a rule follower. Once, when he was a freshman in high school, I found two containers of keyboard duster in his room. I showed the cans to Jeff.

"It's probably just for cleaning his keyboard," Jeff told me.

"Do you think? Why would he have two containers of it? And he bought it himself, rather than asking me to get it for him," I said.

After discussing it, we concluded that surely our very bright son would have more sense than to huff this stuff. Even so, I tucked both containers away in Jeff's closet. When we asked Sam about the cans, he seemed indignant that we would suggest that he would do such a stupid thing. We wanted to believe him; he had never given us any reason not to trust him. Still, I kept the duster spray hidden. He didn't ask for it back.

I WAS PAINED when Sam was suspended over the homecoming voting incident.

It was a Thursday morning in the fall of Sam's sophomore year in high school, and I was filling my water jug in the kitchen sink in preparation for meeting friends to play doubles tennis when the phone rang. It was one of the assistant principals at Sam's high school. She told me that Sam was going to be suspended for bullying and computer trespassing.

"I'm sorry," I told her, "but you cannot be talking about my son, Sam Owen. Have you checked his record?"

"Yes, ma'am, he's a brilliant boy, and he's made a big mistake."

As she explained to me how my son had illegally infiltrated the school's computer system to change the votes for homecoming king, I felt the blood rush from my face. I was at a loss. The bullying charge deeply troubled me. I'd always viewed my son as being one of the kindest people I'd ever known. The assistant principal gave me the option of leaving Sam at school that day for in-school suspension or picking him up. I told her, keep him, I'd see him when he got home. It was my idea of tough love, I guess.

I worried and fretted for most of the day. I felt certain Sam had given up his future for some lark. I worried colleges would consider this stunt a reason to reject him. At three o'clock, I heard him walk in from the bus. I waited for him to find me on the sofa in our family room. "How was your day?" I asked. My voice was sardonic—I wanted him to know that I knew—but I think it was probably also obvious to him that I had been crying.

"I'm sorry," he told me. His demeanor and voice indicated his true regret.

He said he'd never meant to bully the kid. Instead, he told me, he had been trying to draw attention to the meaninglessness of homecoming royalty. This "radical thinking" resonated perfectly with my beliefs about such archaic, sexist traditions, and Sam knew it. Still, I hated that he had taken the risk of hacking the school's computer system.

Jeff liked to tell people that after this event, I took to bed for two days, crying about it. I didn't, but it's true that I was upset. I was invested in Sam and in his future, so much so that I could not stand a blight on his school record. Looking back, I should have focused more on the fact that this incident gave Sam a valuable lesson. His actions were not a direct reflection on me. He was becoming his own individual, figuring things out—sometimes the hard way.

For the remaining three days of in-home suspension, Jeff set Sam to work on an outdoor project in our yard—digging a trench to contain a runoff pipe from our air conditioning system. As for me, I began my work with the high school administration. I emailed the assistant principal and told her other students would admit that the kid who had acquired the extra votes had been in on the prank. My initial emails to her went unanswered. However, once I got the main principal involved, they interviewed the student who Sam had rigged the vote for. This boy confirmed that he knew about it and didn't feel Sam was making fun of him. The bullying charge was dropped. The computer trespassing charge, however, would remain. A resource officer read Sam the riot act, telling Sam that if he were seventeen instead of fifteen, he could have been brought up on national and international charges of computer trespassing. Sam told us this was a big wakeup call for him.

AT THE BEGINNING of his senior year of high school, Sam tried to break out of his shell. He started feeling more confident and asking girls out. He dated a couple of girls, but there was one he was particularly infatuated with. He had tried to be generous and inventive with dates — going to museums and well-reviewed restaurants. After going out a few times, it became clear that the girl did not return his affection. She was not unkind about it, telling Sam she liked him but didn't have time for a relationship then. She said she needed to concentrate on school and college applications.

When he told me about the rejection, he relayed the news matter-of-factly, but I could tell he was sad. I hurt for Sam, but I thought he was taking the rebuff in stride. I came to find out that wasn't true when one Friday, not long after, I walked by Sam's bedroom while he was at school and found he had smashed a collage that hung on his wall. I had made the collage from pictures of Sam at different stages of his life. The photos were ripped and the frames broken. He had destroyed the collage with such force that even the wall had been damaged. My heart sank.

Standing in the doorway, still staring at the mess in his room, I phoned him. I asked if he was okay and if I should come get him. He said he was okay and would talk with me when he got home. He seemed chagrined and not annoyed that I was checking on him.

I was jittery with worry until he came home after school, skipping swim practice. We stood in the kitchen as he confessed to me that he was upset about the rejection from this girl and had taken a handful of Benadryl the night before. I asked him if this was an attempted suicide, but his response was no. He just did not want to be sober, and that was all he had been able to find.

Sam said the antihistamine had stayed in his system throughout the day, making him act strangely and speak oddly to others. I was a tiny bit dubious that it was indeed Benadryl that had made him react like this, but I didn't voice my doubts.

"Mom, I don't know what's wrong with me," he said.

Sam told me that he felt he didn't fit in well in this world. He said he didn't understand why now, being a senior in high school, he could not get excited about his future.

That admission opened a dialogue between us about his depression. I felt my heart go heavy, even as I tried to convey some optimism. I said that there was nothing abnormal about having depression. I told him that teenage depression is extremely common and recounted an article I had read in *National Geographic* that indicated that girls get their sense of self-esteem from other girls while boys also get theirs from girls. I told him this was a false indicator and he should not fall into this trap.

Sam listened to me but gave few verbal or nonverbal cues indicating whether he believed this. I told him that we would get him help. To this he simply said, "Okay. Thanks." His face then softened, giving off a sense of relief, and I felt like he had been wanting to talk with me about his depression for some time. I felt part of that burden he carried transfer to me. With sadness, I accepted this new reality and began to try to get Sam help.

SAM, JEFF, AND I had lunch at a local deli the next day, Saturday. Together we discussed Sam's feelings and actions. Jeff again asked Sam if he had been trying to kill himself, but Sam said no. He had read on the internet about getting high on Benadryl. He did admit that he had done it to mask his emotional pain.

The emotional tone of our conversation was solemn and sincere. We reassured him that we would always be there for him. We asked him to both be honest with us and to lean on us for help. I told him I would make inquiries to find a psychologist, and Sam agreed he would go to therapy.

I contacted friends who I knew to have set up therapy for their own kids and asked for recommendations. The first psychologist I called, who came highly recommended, was not taking any new patients at this time. She recommended another psychologist in the same practice, Dr. R. I called the doctor and set an appointment. The next week, Sam started counseling sessions with this psychologist. He saw Dr. R. bi-weekly for the remainder of his senior year and throughout the following summer. After the first session, Sam said he liked Dr. R. He found him both smart and easy to talk with. Sam said he gave him good advice. I was glad, and relieved, to hear that Sam felt like psychotherapy was going to be a positive experience.

The Benadryl overdose scared me, and, accordingly, I took some additional precautions to help protect Sam. Jeff has some hunting rifles inherited from his grandfather. They were in Jeff's closet, hidden but not under lock and key. After I asked, Jeff bought a safe to put them in. In one of the cabinets at the end of an antique buffet in our dining room, we have a makeshift liquor cabinet containing mostly liqueurs. Neither Jeff nor I had ever advertised this to the kids, so I'm not sure whether Sam even knew of its existence then. But along with the bottles of Grand Marnier and Chambord was a bottle of absinthe, given to us by Jeff's brother for Christmas. Absinthe is bottled with a range of alcohol between 45 and 75 percent. I asked Jeff if he minded if I got rid of it. He didn't, and I poured the green liquid down the kitchen drain.

IN THE FOLLOWING weeks, from our vantage point, psychotherapy seemed to be working for Sam. He was happy to have a neutral party to discuss feelings with. He became more engaged with friends and more motivated in his college search.

In early October, Sam began his fourth year of swimming on the high school varsity team. One day that fall, he came into my home office with a question on his mind.

"Would it be okay if I practiced with Swim Atlanta this year instead of with the team?" he asked. Swim Atlanta has eight pool facilities in the Atlanta area and has turned out Olympic athletes, including Amanda Weir, who medaled in both the 2004 and 2012 games. Sam had participated in swimming lessons and swim team at Swim Atlanta on and off since elementary school.

He told me that this season he really wanted to make the cut to go to the state championships, since he hadn't before. Sam had made the All-County Team and lettered each of the three years prior but had yet to make the state cut. He wanted to renew his membership at Swim Atlanta and swim there the rest of the year to improve his times. The intensive instruction and expectation at Swim Atlanta promised faster times than if he only practiced with his high school team. I agreed. If $200 a month would help him achieve a goal and give him a sense of worthiness, it would be money well spent.

Sam worked hard that swim season, going to Swim Atlanta five days a week and lifting weights in our basement three to four times a week. I admired his tenacity and his focus on his goal. I felt like striving for a state qualifying time was a good sign, given his admission of depression just one month earlier. I prayed that his hard work would result in his goal—making the state team. Throughout the season, his times improved. The stroke he concentrated on was the 200-yard individual medley (IM), in which the swimmer crosses a 25-yard pool twice for each stroke: butterfly, backstroke, breaststroke, and freestyle. One reason he focused on the IM was because it is both a speed and endurance event. Like me, Sam had slow-twitch, as opposed to fast-twitch, muscle fibers—facilitating endurance over speed. Sam made the county cut within the first two weeks of the season, but going into the last meet of the regular season, he still had not made the state cut.

The last meet was a night meet. Jeff was out of town, but Claire and I went. Besides IM, Sam also swam the 100-yard butterfly event and 100-yard breaststroke event that night.

As Sam finished his breaststroke, he popped out of the pool. The stroke-and-turn judge raised a card indicating a disqualification. The judge disqualified Sam because he had taken an extra pull at the end in trying to beat his time. Sam exited the pool, nodded to the judge, and started walking back to join his team at the other end of the pool. The judge was not finished with him, though, and told him to come back and talk to him.

Sam looked over his shoulder and said, "Yeah, man, I got it. I know what I did."

The judge grabbed Sam's shoulder to turn him around. Sam jerked his shoulder away and gave the judge the middle finger.

Unfortunately for Sam, one of his assistant principals, Mr. S., was standing poolside. "Let's go!" Mr. S. said angrily. He escorted Sam into a room at the pool complex and went to get the head coach, who told Mr. S. that Sam was his athlete and that he would handle the situation.

Sam's coach showed mercy on him. Normally, such an infraction would result in a one-meet suspension. But the only meet left was the county meet, Sam's last chance to make state. Coach E. did not suspend Sam. He told him he needed to write a letter of apology to the stroke-and-turn judge. Sam thanked the coach and wrote the letter the next day.

I had left the meet before all this had happened. When Sam told me the story later, I felt frustrated and annoyed that he had acted so rashly and angrily—but, then again, that was another way he and I could be alike. Sam told me that he had gotten a lucky break in not being suspended from the upcoming meet.

At the county meet the following week, Jeff and I were so on edge that we couldn't stand next to one another. Jeff made his way up to a higher bleacher, and Claire and I stood tensely with other swim parents on a lower level, hoping and praying that he would make the state cut (a time of 2:12:00 or better). As Sam dove off the block, I watched the timer on the jumbotron, noting the splits between each stroke. I could hardly breathe when he touched the pool's edge at the end of his last lap. 2:10:86. He had made the cut.

I hugged Claire hard. I hugged other swim parents around me. I was thrilled for Sam, and I believed that, for one of the few times in his life, he was also proud of himself.

ACADEMICALLY, SAM SAILED through high school, taking the hardest classes while being on the varsity swim team. He took fourteen Advanced Placement classes and, during his senior year, took Calculus I and II from Georgia Tech. He did well on standardized tests, scoring 35 out of 36 on the ACT. He applied for early admission and was accepted at Georgia Tech, entering as a sophomore, since he had earned 33 credit hours from Advanced Placement tests. We were happy with the news, but Sam still wanted to apply to a few other "dream schools": Harvard, Yale, Columbia, and UPenn. In late fall 2013, I took him to New York to visit Columbia University. (Jeff would then take Sam to visit UPenn in December.)

Our trip to NYC got off to a rough start. We had made it through the jungle that is the TSA checkpoint in Atlanta's airport and were on our way to the gate when Sam suddenly realized he did not have his phone. Panic ensued. He went back to TSA, but it wasn't there. He went back to our car to check. He walked all the way to the airport parking garage and searched the car for his phone. The minutes were ticking by, and the plane had started boarding. Sam did not find his phone in the car, and I couldn't call him, obviously.

I went to the desk at our gate and was told we could take a later flight. That was a relief, but I was still anxious because Sam was taking a long time to get to the gate. Of course, he had to come back through TSA. As Delta called "last call" to board the flight, I saw Sam walking toward me, matter-of-factly, with his hands in his pockets. I yelled, "Run, Sam, run!"

He ran, and we made the flight. We both had a good time in New York; it was Sam's first trip to the city. It was a struggle keeping track of one another without a phone for Sam. He also would get frustrated with me for not understanding walking directions from Google Maps. I led us down the wrong route frequently. Still, we managed. (Of course, after we arrived back in Atlanta, we found the phone tucked into the crevice of the passenger seat.)

On the last day of the trip, while still at the hotel, Sam earnestly told me, "Mom, I'm glad we could make this trip together." Then he gave me the best hug. Other parents of teenagers can attest to the fact that a hug initiated by a teenager is a kind of secular miracle.

IN EARLY MARCH 2014, as Sam's senior year was drawing to a close, my dad had a heart attack. I immediately went to west Tennessee to stay for three weeks. He had successful quadruple bypass surgery and eventually made a full recovery. I was still in Tennessee, driving from my parents' home to the hospital for a visit, when Sam called to say he hadn't gotten into any of the Ivies. I knew he was crushed. I felt I needed to be with him, knowing his innate capacity for self-blaming.

I called Jeff, who said Sam seemed to be handling the situation. As the evening wore on, I kept texting Sam; mostly, he did not reply. I wanted him to know this rejection did not define him. He had already been accepted to Georgia Tech, entering as a *sophomore*, and there was no reason he couldn't consider a transfer to an Ivy or attend one for graduate school. I sent him an article that said that kids who are willing to put themselves out there by applying to the Ivies will be successful. Only the best and the brightest would even apply. I sent him a second article I found stating that Georgia Tech ranked first as far as being a better bang for the buck than the Ivies. To this text, Sam quickly responded with "TLDR." I had to look that acronym up online. In text-speak, it means "Too long; didn't read." I could tell from that four-letter text that he had no interest in my attempts to cheer him. Sam would not talk about his sadness over being rejected. He internalized this letdown and added it to his long list of perceived failures.

Moving forward, the business of senior year kept him occupied. That spring, the swim team held its senior banquet. Jeff, Sam, and I went to the event, which was held at a local Italian restaurant. Each senior gave a short speech, thanking their coaches and parents and saying what a great experience the swim team had been. Sam, instead, took the floor as though it were open-mic night at a comedy club. His speech had his teammates, the coaches, and the parents laughing. I appreciated Sam's dry, sarcastic wit, and I was happy to see that this crowd appreciated it too.

There was prom, and then graduation. His graduation party was attended mostly by my friends. He kept saying it was a party for me and not him. I encouraged him to invite his friends, too. He asked a couple of them to come, and later, after attending other friends' parties, said he regretted that he hadn't asked more. We ate a catered meal of barbeque and sides as well as beer, wine, and soft drinks. Many of the guests stayed inside the house while others spilled out onto our deck and backyard. I think Sam enjoyed it. He interacted easily with the adults. I was beginning to see him as no longer my "boy," but as a young man. And I was proud to be his mom.

There was an annual tradition at Sam's high school of asking friends and family to write personal messages of encouragement and congratulations to their graduate. The letters are sent directly to the school and then given to the graduates in individual folders at their Senior Breakfast. When Sam received his, he did not want me to read the letters. Later, though, of course, I would see them. Here is a portion of what Maggie wrote to Sam:

Sam, I wish you luck as you're on your way to college. Surely, I, a thirteen-year-old cannot offer you any advice. You are by far one of the smartest people I know. You are going to be great someday. "It's in the bag."

I just want you to know it will be hell without you here. Mom will go crazy. How will she deal with Claire and me by herself? I don't know how we'll get along without you. Now every time Dad needs help lifting something heavy, who will help him? Not Claire, that's for sure. Who will be there to help me with my homework? Who will be there to correct my grammar? You have probably already found several mistakes in this letter by now!

I don't mean any of these things to come off as me being self-ish…. This is just my way of telling you how great you are! After high school and college, you begin your new life, but please don't forget your old one. ~Maggie

Maggie's "in the bag" comment was a reference to how she had encouraged Sam at different times. Maggie was eleven when Jeff took Sam to get his driver's license. As Sam was leaving the house, she said, "You can do this, Sam. It's in the bag!" She told me once that she reserved that phrase of encouragement for when she knew Sam most needed a boost of confidence.

THE SUMMER AFTER graduation, Sam went to Forbach, a township on the border of France and Germany, to stay with a host family. This was a school-planned activity, and he traveled with fellow AP French students and his teacher. Sam was quite taken by the lifestyle of his host family and said he much preferred this area to Paris. Toward the end of his stay, during a Skype conversation, he said, "Mom, I miss my family."

"Oh, Sam, we miss you, too."

"Oh, not you guys," came his rapid rejoinder. "I mean my French family." He softened this by saying he'd see us the rest of his life, but not his French family, with whom he had parted earlier that day.

I always thought Sam would end up studying or working in Europe. He gravitated toward the European lifestyle. I didn't mind the thought of living an ocean away from him because I knew he would always stay connected with us, and because I wanted him to fulfill his dreams. Sam had told me his life's dreams included extensive travel, humanitarian work, and bettering the world through scientific discovery.

Once he returned from France, however, Sam seemed to be at loose ends in keeping himself occupied. He delivered pizzas, played video games, watched Netflix on his computer, and smoked a good bit of weed. Jeff and I confronted him several times and asked that he not smoke at home. I told Sam that his younger sisters were not equipped to handle his exploration of marijuana. Rather than stopping, he began to hide his habit better. I did several searches of his room and removed any bong or other paraphernalia I found.

Looking back, I believe we should have been stricter with him about his marijuana use. I mistakenly thought then that pot was no worse than drinking alcohol. During this time, I didn't realize that the marijuana of today is much more potent than ever. In fact, the level of THC in marijuana tripled between 1995 and 2014. I could always tell when Sam was stoned—his eyelids would slightly droop over his reddened eyes; he smiled more, and he spoke more slowly. Frustrated, I remember declaring to him that summer, "Sam, you are off the rails!"

"Mom, I can't even *find* the rails," he told me.

"I know you think that's funny, but it isn't. You need to cut down on your smoking."

"Your wine will kill you long before weed kills me."

I've heard other parents say that by the time kids go off to college, moms, dads, and kids are all ready for a little separation. I began to understand that feeling. Maybe it was time for a break from the day-to-day mothering.

He continued psychotherapy, and the therapist told us he was not overly concerned about Sam's pot use. And, ultimately, I believed in Sam's character and never really thought that pot would lead to any other drug issues or lapses in his education. Beyond all else, I knew how driven Sam was to succeed. I was also confident he knew how much he meant to his family and would never willingly hurt us by becoming an addict.

I STILL HAVE a copy of the speech Sam made at his senior banquet for the swim team, the one that left his teammates in fits of laughter. Reading now, I can still smile at Sam's great wit, though the last paragraph always breaks my heart.

> In cliché fashion, I would like to open with a quote. This one happens to be by Michael Dell. I guess he made computers and stuff.
>
> Anyways, it goes, "Try never to be the smartest person in the room. And if you are, I suggest you invite smarter people… or find a different room." But I'll stick around. It's a silly quote, really, because the first person would need to leave and then the next person and so on. I don't even know why I brought it up.
>
> It's been a long four years. Well, actually, they've all been the standard 365, but you know what I mean. Through this experience, I have discovered a great deal about myself, like… well, I have. I promise. Shouts out to my coaches and everyone who has made this experience possible—and the teammates who have made it bearable. You guys are… eh… acceptable.
>
> As I close this chapter of my life, I look ahead to the future, and I would advise all of you to do the same. And be jealous of my awesome future. And now, I need to find a different room.

Sam at the county swim meet, 2014

Sam, Nina, and teammate at county swim meet

Sam giving his speech at the swim team Senior Banquet

Charles, Kat, Katie, and Sam — Prom 2014

Nina, Jeff, and Sam at Sam's Graduation Party

Host family kids with Sam and Devin, his classmate

CHAPTER 9

Freshman Year at Georgia Tech

On August 14, 2014, Jeff and I helped move Sam into his dorm at Georgia Tech. The campus was abuzz with freshman move-in day. The streets and sidewalks in front of the dorms were crowded with kids and their parents carrying boxes and calling out to each other.

Sam's room was in Hanson Hall—a dorm specifically for first-year students. His roommate was also named Sam. As we entered the room, our Sam walked over to his roommate and extended his hand, introducing himself. The other Sam, Sam P., was sitting at his desk, playing a video game. He ignored Sam's attempt at a handshake and, still looking at his computer screen, muttered his name.

"Sam, where are you from?" I tried.

"Georgia."

Okay, well, that narrows it down! It was like pulling teeth. Eventually we found out that Sam P. was from a small town in northwest Georgia.

Jeff, Sam, and I headed out to our minivan to begin to unload Sam's things. The heaviest item was a small refrigerator. Other than that, Sam had packed modestly. As he'd pointed out, since he was only forty-five minutes from home, he could easily get anything else he might need.

Back in the room, I attempted to put a small rug in the space between the roommates' beds and desks. Sam P. would not get out of his desk chair, preventing me from arranging the rug evenly.

Later, when we were alone, Jeff said to me, "I don't really like that kid." I agreed. He seemed odd. At the very least, he was extraordinarily introverted and socially awkward.

In the ensuing weeks, Sam tried to engage his roommate, asking him to go grab a meal or do something else small around the campus, but Sam P. mostly would not even acknowledge that Sam was speaking to him. Sam told me he had hoped for a different kind of freshman roommate bonding experience, but he eventually became indifferent toward Sam P. and found his friends elsewhere.

Freshmen at Georgia Tech are required to move in a week earlier than other classes. With little else to do, Sam attended a few fraternity rush parties. He was offered two bids and selected one. When he told me that he was pledging, I was dumbstruck. Sam had always been independent and quietly resistant to authority. I could not fathom him in a fraternity. Still, we supported his decision to pledge — Sam was the one in the situation, not us, and we felt he better knew the variables that had gone into his decision. I thought he needed friends and a social life to have an outlet from the strenuous academics at Georgia Tech.

I think Sam enjoyed the fraternity at first. He told us about the racial diversity of the brothers and other positive things about them. But things quickly went sideways. As most college fraternities do, they treated the pledges like garbage. Sam told one story about being made to clean up a brother's vomit. That was the beginning of the end. Sam stopped hanging out at the house and didn't make much of an effort to participate in the frat activities. During the middle of the semester, he was dropped from the fraternity. The following weekend, Sam called Jeff and asked to come home. Sam did not have his car at Tech and was dependent upon us for transportation to and from home. When he got to our house, he told me the story of being dropped by the fraternity. I could see that even though he knew the frat was not a good fit for him, getting dumped was upsetting. A rejection. A loss. Someone saying he wasn't good enough. One more blow to his fragile self-confidence.

I told him he was far too good to participate in "rent-a-friend" Greek life. Later, though, I went to my room and cried, silently asking God why my kid could not catch a break to build his self-esteem. I hurt for Sam considerably. He truly needed a social win.

THAT SAME SEMESTER, Sam had a run-in with the campus police. He was away at an on-campus party but had a six-pack of beer in the refrigerator of his room. His roommate, Sam P., found the beer and panicked and called the Georgia Tech police. The police called Sam to come back to his dorm. Sam said that when he got there, the two police officers—almost apologetically—looked into his refrigerator and took the six-pack of beer. One of the policemen wondered aloud why the roommate had not gone to the R.A. with this instead of to the GTPD. Even so, the officer issued a citation. Sam was required to write a reflection piece on the episode before going in front of the housing board to plead his case.

SAM'S REFLECTION PAPER for the housing board is another one of his writings I still have. In the essay, Sam's trademark dry humor and mistrust of the status quo is on full display. In a section of it he wrote:

> *It is clearly stated in Georgia Tech's housing contract, titled "Technically Speaking," that possession of alcohol by a minor is strictly prohibited.*
>
> *Therefore, as an individual under the legal drinking age, it is no surprise that I faced disciplinary actions when the Georgia Tech Police Department found alcohol in my refrigerator. As I am not twenty-one years old, the possession of such substance is explicitly disallowed, and although I knew this information, I persisted for several reasons.*
>
> *First of all, I was only holding the alcohol in the refrigerator temporarily and planned to relocate it later in the evening. Second,*

I had the door locked and did not expect anybody to be in my room until much later. And finally, I imagined that if somebody did know of the alcohol and were bothered by it, he or she would contact me to resolve the issue rather than immediately calling campus police.

However, I forgot to account for one possibility: my roommate having a seizure-induced panic attack, resulting in him calling the police. I realize now that I was foolish to believe that I could avoid the consequences of an act as dangerous as the possession of a six-pack of Sierra Nevada Extra Pale Ale. I should be thankful that campus police were able to intervene, for if I had consumed the alcohol, according to the My Student Body online course, I would have engaged in even riskier behavior which potentially could have led to conflict, damage to persons or property, or questionable sexual decisions.

To avoid any future violations, I should not keep alcohol in my room, especially in a location as obvious as a refrigerator. I should also avoid the residence hall while intoxicated, as this could lead to a violation as well, especially if I behave in a disorderly manner.

Sam told Jeff and me about the incident when we took him to dinner at JCT Kitchen in Atlanta on his nineteenth birthday. He said he was angry at his roommate for turning him in to the police. We agreed that Sam P. displayed curious social anomalies.

I was glad Sam had told us and appreciated that he felt secure in knowing we would not overreact to the infraction. I took this latest lapse of judgment lightly. Since Sam had moved away to college, my mothering had started to move from "quasi-helicopter mom" to more of a role as a consultant and supporter. I felt like the best thing I could do for him now was further a relationship of mutual respect.

During that dinner, Sam also updated us on his feelings about his major, telling us that he was beginning to question his choice of aeronautical engineering. Sam had been permitted to enroll in only one AE class during his first semester. He had signed up for additional AE classes second semester, but, early into this term, he'd told us that "This is not for me; these are not my people." After meeting with his counselor, he switched his major to physics, for which he had an innate ability. Jeff and I were supportive of his decision. We wanted him to really like what he was studying. We always felt that with his innate intelligence and curiosity, he would continue to graduate school after earning an undergraduate degree.

When he was young, when anyone asked him what he wanted to be when he grew up, Sam always answered, "I want to be a hobo with a Ph.D."

DURING HIS FIRST semester, Sam had come home often on the weekends. But now, during spring semester, he began staying at school more often. Over the high school's spring break, Maggie and I went to France, and Jeff booked a camping and horseback excursion for Claire and himself. The girls' spring break was over the Easter holidays. Sam's spring break had been a few weeks earlier.

When I told Sam of our plans, he hesitated and then said, "Wait, I'm going to be alone on Easter?"

I felt an immediate sense of guilt, but I honestly hadn't considered that he'd be stuck on campus on a holiday weekend. Our family was churchgoing, but sporadically at best. Still, I got his point. Most of the students would be with family, and he wouldn't be. I told him I really hadn't thought he would mind, and, of course, he then said he didn't. I wish now I had paid more attention and had at least had the courtesy to let him know about the trips before everything was finalized. He must have been planning to spend the holiday weekend with us.

After we returned from our respective trips, Sam was approaching the last weeks before his final exams. With studying to do and papers to write, he had little time to speak with us or answer texts. One text he did answer was when I let him know that a letter had arrived for him from California. I asked him if he wanted me to open it. He quickly responded and said no, that he was expecting it, and that it was regarding a physics scholarship he'd applied for. It looked official to me, and I left the envelope on my desk until he moved back home for the summer. Months later, Sam confessed that the envelope had contained LSD.

CHAPTER 10

Sam's Writing

Found in Google Docs: "Fear and Loathing in Midtown Atlanta"

*S*o, I took acid and went with these Hanson people to the High Museum. I can't write very well because I'm coming off an acid trip so please excuse the lack of this document making any sense.

What actually happened:

- *We walked to a Panera Bread*
- *I ordered a bagel (it was cheap) and had no idea what to do with it because I was on acid.*
- *There was this pretentious Dutch guy who sat across from me who subtly flexed the branding on his Ralph Lauren wallet. This kid literally put his wallet on the table, so we could see its branding. Granted, he did attempt some subtlety in covering most of it with his scarf.*
- *We moved throughout the museum noting the art.*
- *We stepped outside for a smoke, and during our four-cigarette session, we noted an awkward couple, probably a first date. The guy wanted a hookup or something with the girl, an absurd expectation considering how inconducive the atmosphere was to any kind of romantic prospect. (sketchy MARTA station on a rainy night LMFAO). But hey, the thirst is real, ya know?*
- *After coming back inside, we met a guy who we talked to at Phi Kap last night, but he was with other friends, so we kept the interaction brief.*

- *We moved through the museum some more, not really settling anywhere for too long. My associate noted interest in visiting the Hill Auditorium, so I went along, not really knowing what-was-what at the time.*
- *A security guard directed us to go past an emergency exit to enter the auditorium, that was kind of sketchy, in and of itself.*
- *Apparently, there was supposed to be a screening of something from 8 to 12; but the auditorium was entirely void, minus the one woman who worked there who seemed a bit confused by our presence.*
- *We went back, noted the band playing, and otherwise mulled about amidst the dwindling crowd.*
- *The group then met up, and we began working out our departure. A few people drove back, and we were left with the same crew that we walked to the museum with, minus the 7/10 PL broad.*
- *My associate and I just followed the rest of the squad, and it soon became apparent that they had no idea where they were going.*
- *Humorously, the MARTA station in question was the same location where we had taken the cig break, but being on drugs, we had forgotten all about that.*
- *While we were waiting on the train, I wandered off, hoping to get away from the painfully phony Hanson crew. Noticing another woman smoking, I took the opportunity to smoke another cig to help quell the acid-induced restlessness. After getting a light from the woman (my lighter was with my associate), I was made aware of the buzz surrounding something called the "Icy Hot Challenge."*
- *Incidentally, the rest of the crew followed and caught me smoking, that felt a little awkward. I doubt they actually cared, but the drug I was on made it seem so. Interestingly enough, I did notice that they appeared a little less open to interaction following that. Considering the natures of those people, it would not surprise me if their opinion of me sunk a bit.*
- *Walking out of MARTA, we went into a Goodfellas and bid farewell to the remainder of the group.*
- *And now I'm here, trying to make sense of it all.*

Interactions that stood out to me:

- *The majors talk between the Dutch guy and me*
  - *Me: So, what are you planning to do with an ME [mechanical engineering] degree since it's so broad?*
  - *Him: I was hoping to work.*
  - *The way he said that definitely came off as a sneer toward me being a physics major. That might not actually be the case since I was on acid and was predisposed to expect hostility in interacting with someone with whom I was unfamiliar.*
- *Smalltalk in the booth at Panera*
  - *So, in my confusion at the bagel, the pretentious guy said something along the lines of "Have you never seen a bagel with cream cheese?" I responded that I was of humble origins and expected it to be pre-cut. He then made some plug about smoked salmon and capers. Again, trying so hard to be sophisticated. Smoked salmon and fucking capers. Is this guy for real?*
  - *When the topic of music came up, I noted the generic "anything but metal" response.*
- *Me accidentally hitting on the Hanson PL*
  - *Her asking if we had her number and me responding with a matter of fact "no" may have communicated that I wanted her number or something like that.*
  - *As we were all leaving, I noted that she was violating my personal space a bit, and I picked up a sense of expectation from her. However, since I was on acid, I immediately was put on edge, and she backed off.*
  - *This is probably just me reading too much into the situation due to my own vanity and the drug I was on.*
- *The Asian girls we briefly met*
  - *Introduced ourselves, but they were acting awkward because we were out of their league. Still, we felt like we had said or done something wrong to create the awkwardness because of the fucking ratio, man. In reality, there was nothing socially abnormal*

that we did, but we were predisposed to suspect our own failure to communicate. Furthermore, they were from UGA, where the ratio works in the opposite direction, thus helping to explain their nervousness about being approached.

Overarching Concepts of the Trip and other Miscellaneous Thoughts:

- Don't follow the crowd. Immerse yourself in what truly impassions you, and the crowd will follow.
- The fundamental difference between the drugs we were on (Xan & acid) meant that we found ourselves wanting to do different things (talking to people vs. tripping out while looking at a painting)
- Nobody at the museum seemed to give a shit about the art itself. The average person there appeared to be one-half of an awkward first date. It's funny because you would take somebody to an art museum to convey a sense of sophistication. But it became painfully obvious how unaware these people were to the art itself. Like what the actual fuck? Why does society attribute an appreciation of visual art to sophistication while simultaneously disregarding artistic expression amidst the minutia of everyday life?
- Most people with whom I interacted were putting up a massive front. While erecting a facade of elegance, they neglected the essence of elegance itself.
- Interacting in social situations wasn't as difficult as I expected considering how fucked-up I was.
- Nobody in the group seemed to have any actual interest in the event and were merely showing up in support of a friend.
- There was this garish umbrella that we kept getting stuck with (it belonged to that Asian girl). Whenever it was in my possession, I became preoccupied with getting rid of it by means of finding a socially acceptable way to pass it off.
- Writing is fun; I should do it more.

Questions

- *What is sophistication?*
  - *There is no archetypal answer that I know of; however, what I observed in the High Museum of Art was anything but.*
- *Why does society deem certain pursuits to be sophisticated over others?*
- *Has the prevalence of sophistication as a driving force in everyday life decreased?*

CHAPTER 11

Summer 2015

In May 2015, Sam came home for the summer after completing his first year at Tech. I could tell he was depressed. He told us that he was not happy to be back living in Suwanee, but that he couldn't think of a viable alternative. He couldn't afford rent on an Atlanta apartment, and he needed to save money for the fall semester. Even though he did go out occasionally with friends, if he was home, he was in the basement playing video games or watching movies. When he was around us, he seemed restless and discontented.

He had been home only a couple of weeks when I became concerned enough to ask him about it. I felt like his depression was more than a typical case of "teen angst."

I was standing alone in the kitchen doing dishes when Sam came upstairs to look for something to eat. He stared into the pantry for a full thirty seconds without selecting anything.

"What's going on, Sam? You seem down," I said.

He shrugged and walked over to our kitchen island and leaned against it. "I feel like nothing in my life is right. I have almost no social life."

"But, Sam, I've met your friends," I countered. "You have plenty of friends from high school and in college." He hadn't mentioned to either me or Jeff that he was seeing anyone, and I thought perhaps a lack of dating was contributing to his low feelings. I asked him if he was seeing anyone.

He shrugged.

I reminded Sam that Georgia Tech was a tougher atmosphere for boys, dating-wise. Sixty percent of Tech students were male. I also told him that, when it came to friendships, quality over quantity should be his goal. As I said this to Sam, I hoped he would listen and believe and hurt less. I wanted him to suffer less and not be so hard on himself. Nevertheless, I felt my words were futile and falling flat. His depressive state would not allow him to take in anything encouraging.

"Yeah, well, also, for the first time in my life, I'm questioning my intellect. I'm beginning to think I'm just an average student."

"I promise, you are not. Tech is a tough school."

I tried to assuage him by saying that if Tech was not the right place, there was nothing wrong with making a change. He could transfer to a variety of other schools, but he needed to be the one to take the initiative. With his depression, however, he didn't have the energy to even begin. When he'd started college, Jeff and I had encouraged him to participate in one of the study-abroad programs Tech offered. I knew he enjoyed Europe and believed he would flourish there. But he never applied.

THROUGHOUT HIS FRESHMAN year, Sam had maintained the required GPA (3.3 or higher) to keep his scholarship—which paid 100 percent of his tuition. At Tech, studying science and engineering, that is no small feat. His cumulative GPA after the fall semester was 3.63. However, in the spring semester, he earned his first C ever—in Dynamics. This and a couple of Bs lowered his cumulative GPA to 3.4.

One day in May, at the end of his second semester, Sam came to Jeff and me about his grades, chagrined. I told him that I thought his grades were fine. Sensing Sam's angst about the matter, Jeff shared with him that he had also received a C in Dynamics from the University of Alabama engineering school. He told Sam to not worry about this one C, that he was doing well and needed to give himself a break.

I chimed in with, "It'll be better next year when you are studying classes pertaining to your physics major."

"Whatever" was Sam's reply.

We were happy with his grades, but in Sam's mind, he had not done well. For the first time in his life, he was being exposed to academic concepts that he had to work to understand. Tech was chipping away at his self-esteem.

Concerned, I asked if I could make an appointment for him to get a physical check-up. I knew he was not acting like himself, and—in my mind—the first course of action should be a checkup with an internist. Knowing this doctor, I thought she would also be likely to talk to him about his mental health. He said okay, and I set an appointment for him to see my general practitioner. I also asked Sam to schedule some sessions with Dr. R., the psychologist he'd seen during his senior year in high school. When Sam got home from the check-up with the internist, I asked him how he'd liked the doctor.

"I didn't."

"Why not?"

"She hounded me with personal questions and then told me I needed to be on an antidepressant."

"Well, Sam, I trust her," I said. "She tries hard to get to know her patients in order to be the best doctor to them possible. She would not prescribe something unless she really felt there was a need."

Sam showed me the prescription. It was for Lexapro. I encouraged him to give the medication a chance. I offered to take the script to the pharmacy and get it filled.

Because Sam was over 18, the doctor could not call me and tell me her concerns. Later, I would find out that she was worried about his increasing drug use and his dismal feelings about a future.

Sam took one dose of the Lexapro and then declared he did not like the way it made him feel. I pleaded with him to give it more of a try, but he began reciting all the adverse side effects. He had made up his mind, and when Sam made up his mind, there was no changing it.

We knew he was still smoking a lot of pot. I would do regular "recon missions" in the basement and throw out any marijuana or other paraphernalia. I would not have known what LSD was even if it were pasted on a wall in plain sight. At this time, we didn't think he had used anything other than marijuana. I was often angered by his smoking and his ambivalence about our concern. This battle between us added friction to the household. He would be angry if I threw out any of his pot. I asked him time and again to stop smoking in our home and tried to get him to see himself through his sisters' eyes. He seemed to think that they were oblivious to his pot use. They were not.

WE DIDN'T TAKE a family vacation that summer. No one seemed to want to. Sam hung out with friends and worked his part-time job delivering pizzas. It was obvious there was a disconnect between how he felt about himself and his reality. I could sense his agitation, but I justified it by remembering feeling restless when I'd returned home for the summer after my freshman year of college. I hoped it would work itself out.

In August, it was time for him to return to Tech. He would be sharing an on-campus apartment with three friends; each boy would have his own bedroom. I was excited for him and felt this would be a much better living situation than sharing a room with Sam P.

On move-in day, we took Sam to lunch at Taqueria del Sol—his choice. The restaurant offered a relaxed vibe and served tacos and enchiladas. During our meal, he said he was glad to be back in Atlanta. After lunch, we took him back to his apartment. He had no interest in letting us help set up his room or make his bed. He seemed anxious for us to leave. Jeff and I gave him a hug and said goodbye. He seemed ready to take on the new academic year. It was August 16, 2015, a little over six months before he would take his life.

CHAPTER 12

Sam's Writing

From Sam's Journal, Found in Google Docs

Sunday, *8/30/15, 2:00 p.m.*

So, after hearing great things about the effects of micro-dosing LSD, I decided to give it a go. As of late, life has been kind of sucking. Depression and anxiety have sapped whatever enjoyment I could have gotten out of my first two weeks at Tech. I've already lost whatever motivation I had going into this scholastic year. This experiment is a Hail Mary of sorts because if things don't start getting better, then I have no idea what the fuck I'm going to do.

I was inspired to try micro-dosing in response to the vast amount of positive feedback regarding it circulating around in internet drug culture. People heralded it as a non-addictive Adderall substitute with tendencies to induce creative thought and heighten empathy. In other words, something too good to be true. The promise of this turning my life around seemed so intense that I held off taking the antidepressant, that I desperately needed, prescribed to me previously last month, as it would reduce the effects of the L.

I was home that weekend, as depression and anxiety oft make me want to leave campus. And I had an intimidatingly large amount of homework to do before the following day.

Before writing this, I took a 125mg tab and cut it into four pieces. Due to the imprecision of my cutting (I blame the dull scissors) the dose I took could range between 20 and 30 mg. As a side note, from now on when I micro-dose, I should drop a tab in a bottle of water and drink a specific volume of it instead of trying to cut it. I'll update as I start noticing the effects. In the meantime, I'm going to put on some DS2 and try to fix a button on my pants.

3:00 p.m. (T+1 hour)
Up until a few minutes ago, I was beginning to worry that I was just experiencing a placebo, but now I can feel the acid kicking in with certainty. Despite being a bit sick, I feel remarkably energetic and positive. Of course, that could also be attributed to an extent to the couple of mugs of hot tea I just drank, but I'm like 95% sure it's the acid. The feeling reminds me of a 10mg dose of Adderall. Unlike the amphetamine, that makes me feel robotic and one-dimensional, this feels more natural, creative, even. The world was amazing, and I was still functional enough to do homework, that I believe I did rather well during that time. The dose, if anything, was too high and the euphoria became rather distracting at times, and I spent probably as much time pacing around my basement as actually doing homework. But more importantly, the drowsy fugue that envelops everyday life had been lifted, and for the first time in several years, I felt optimistic.

4:00 p.m. (T+2 hours)
Definitely feeling it more. It's like the opposite of depression. Instead of wanting to do nothing, I want to do everything. The only thing stopping me from doing homework is the fact that I can't concentrate because of how amazing everything is. For the first time in forever, I'm actually excited and hopeful for the future. It is so fucked how this is a schedule 1 substance. Like I could go to jail for this shit. LMAO

8:30—10:00 p.m.
So, after I got back to campus Sunday, I smoked a couple of cigs, still feeling the effects of the acid, and knowing the cigs would augment my residual high. After my sixth cancer-stick of the evening, I spontaneously decided to quit. After coming to the realization that at my current rate of smoking, addiction was inevitable in the future. Well, I knew that before the moment, but had been apathetic towards the long-term consequences of tobacco due to the assumption that I would OD or suicide long before

lung cancer and shit would matter. Furthermore, I felt a comfort in committing myself toward self-destruction as it is reminiscent of death, for that a significant part of me yearned. So more importantly, rather than contributing to the end of a maladaptive habit, micro-dosing empowered me to feel a will to live.

Monday, 8/31/15

I stayed sober minus my habitual lunchtime PBR and maybe a hit of Xanax (I can't really remember, that probably means I took a Xan. LOL.) The ~30 mg dose I took was apparently too small for an afterglow in the psychological sense, yet I felt uncharacteristically positive and productive. I pretty much spent the day going to class or doing Optics homework, that took forever, but hey, at least I did it, that is better than I would have done most days.

Tuesday, 9/1/15

Today was a good day. Before heading to class, I took what I think was roughly 1/2 to 2/3rds of what I took on Sunday, that is 10-20 mg of California Sunshine. I found myself to be noticeably more engaged and focused in class although my ability to comprehend the material wasn't too affected. (I had hoped the LSD would improve my ability to process and apply complex academics.) This could be because the dose was too low, or I had built up a tolerance, or maybe because Lucy just doesn't work that way. Acid is fickle in the sense that it never does exactly what you want or expect it to do, yet the outcome is almost invariably positive.

During the day, I noticed a significant reduction in my social anxiety and was thus able to be much more conversational and to be present and free of the crushing paranoia that everyone I meet thinks I am weird. In general, I was able to be completely comfortable in my own skin. Which is remarkable for someone with a mind like mine. The anxiety-reduction was better than any number of benzos, alcohol, opiates, or a combination of the three. And, whereas depressants make me feel detached from others, content to immerse myself in the euphoria and nod, micro-dosing amped up my empathy and interest in and connectedness with others big time, thus making me a much more attentive listener. Per consequence of the effects, I had some awesome conversations with people with whom I had previously little connection. During an extended exchange with a classmate, I received a compliment on my outlook on life, that is amazing considering how poor my outlook on life has been for the better part of the past 19 years. And the crazy thing was that I had meant every word of what I said. And the crazier thing is that this was roughly 10 1/2 hours after I had dosed, that is more than enough time for the acid to stop having an effect.

Other cool shit that happened that I'm too lazy to narrate fully:

- Decided to focus on Biophysics
- Found out why Professor Trebino wears a hat (UV protection)
- Noticed some subtle hallucinatory effects (increased color saturation and some noise when I stare at something).
- Also, usual illusions take on an ephemeral weirdness.
- I tended to eat healthier (arugula is great).
- I'm about to go for a run, that would be the first time I've properly exercised in like a year.
- I found it easier to think of things on the fly, like conversation points.
- I cleaned and reorganized my room, creating a little sanctuary devoted to creativity.
- The day seemed prolonged. I felt exhausted after lab, but writing has been reinvigorating.
- As caffeine increases the effects of LSD, coffee has gotten a lot trippier.
- I caught myself smiling a lot more, and even felt downright giddy at times, especially on come up.
- I suspect that the effects of a micro-dose only last ~ 5 hours (can be prolonged by coffee a bit), but the positive energy it gives me kind of carries me through the day.
- In the coming days, I'll try to think of some ways to objectify this experiment to give it a scientific element of validity and precision.
- More precise measurement or dosage

- *Giving days numeric ratings although I'm not keen on this idea*
- *Updating more regularly and more concisely.*

Wednesday, 9/2/15
Schedule for today:

- *Go to class*
- *Do 2232 homework; also stop by SPS room*
- *More class*
- *More homework*
- *Put 'em on wax*
- *Go to CVS to get cash and buy floss and mouthwash and condoms (wishful thinking, lmao) also need wine glasses*
- *More homework, study if time*
- *Go for a run*
- *Look into study-abroad opportunities, undergrad research*

12:00 p.m.
Got back from my run. I puked my guts out, but hey, it only gets better from here! Just took 2.5 mg of Xanax and am going to read a little and pass the fuck out. So, about an hour ago, I was reflecting on the past couple of days and actually cried a tear of joy. It's hard to believe that less than a week ago I wished for death and now I'm living life to the fullest, squeezing as much out of each day as I possibly can. Actually, I can do more, and I will do more, but it's been a hell of a start! :)

6:00 p.m.
I don't really know what to say. From the moment I woke up from the nap, everything just fell apart. And, I got to thinking: why do I even bother? I don't want or need any of this. To what end am I bettering myself or whatever the fuck I like to call it?

On the same page of notebook paper, farther down, Sam wrote:

Fuck it. I quit. Peace out.

To my friends and family, I love you all and wish you the best. This world was not meant to accommodate me. It's no one's fault, just shitty luck, I guess. Stay strong! I know it's an awful thing of me to do to y'all, but it's my life and my choice to end it or not.

The Xanax and whiskey are starting to kick in, so writing doesn't make much sense. I had always wanted a short, witty suicide note, but I guess this lengthy, rambling one will do. You only get one chance at this sort of thing, by definition.

And if someone intervenes, fuck you! Just let me die.

CHAPTER 13

Labor Day Weekend 2015

I spoke to Sam over the phone on Tuesday, September 1. Generally, we communicated via text messaging, but occasionally, I would call him. This time, he was quiet and somewhat unresponsive during our conversation. I asked if he was going to the football game on Thursday evening. Tech was playing in the NCAA season-opening kick-off series. Sam had been a lifelong college football fan, and I knew that normally he would be excited for this game. He seemed ambivalent. I tried asking about the apartment and his roommates and classes. He answered my questions with one-word responses. After just a few minutes, we ended the call.

I tried calling and texting him on Thursday, September 3. I was feeling unsettled about our phone call two days earlier. He didn't respond. Still, I was not overly worried. Sam had always been resistant when I overreached and asked too many questions about how things were going for him.

On the Saturday of Labor Day weekend, September 5, Jeff, Claire, and I went to the greenway near our home to play disc golf. I was particularly bad at the game, but we had fun. While playing, Jeff received a call from Sam. Sam asked Jeff to come to get him at Tech; he wanted to come home.

After the call, I said to Jeff, "Why is he coming home again? He was just here last weekend."

"I'm not going to tell him he can't come home," Jeff said. "I'll go get him."

We wrapped up our game early, and Jeff took Claire and me back to the house before going to pick up Sam. I wasn't concerned about Sam wanting to come home. I thought maybe he needed a quieter place to study.

An hour later, when Jeff and Sam walked in the door to our house, I looked at Sam and immediately felt alarmed. He looked like he had been beaten up. Scrapes and the beginnings of bruises fanned out across his face and arms. His eyes were red, and his body language gave off an air of defeat.

"What happened to you?" I asked.

"Nothing," Sam responded.

"You look like you have been in a fight. Were you mugged?"

"It's nothing. I fell out of my bed."

His answer didn't ring true to me. Yes, his bed was lofted, but what could he possibly have hit in one fall to do that kind of damage to his face?

Sam quickly tired of my questions and said he needed to take a shower. He carried his overnight bag into the basement. I turned my questioning on Jeff. I asked if he had talked to Sam about the bruises and scrapes. Jeff said he hadn't noticed them. I asked him what they had discussed on the ride home. Jeff said not much of anything. He said that the only thing he had asked was why Sam had wanted to come home this weekend; he said Sam had replied that he had cracked the screen on his phone and needed to get it fixed or replaced.

SAM NAPPED AFTER his shower. Around three o'clock, I went downstairs to ask him to watch football with his dad and me. I was feeling some concern for him—his scratches, his body language, his avoidance. I thought watching a game with us might get him out of his funk and inspire him to open up to us about what was going on. He grudgingly agreed and followed me up the stairs.

I sat on the sofa next to him as we watched the Alabama game. I tried again.

"Sam, please tell me what really happened."

He said he'd had too much to drink and passed out, which was how he'd ended up on the floor. Although this was a bad enough scenario, I knew Sam better than anyone, and I could tell that he was holding back. After deflecting my questions for a few minutes, he told me to stop badgering him and went back into the basement.

The next day, Sunday, Jeff took Sam to Costco and paid for him to get a new phone. I fussed a bit about the cost of the new Samsung smartphone. I told Sam he would have to pay for any subsequent devices.

He continued to be sullen and despondent that day. He came upstairs for breakfast—late—and poured himself a bowl of cereal. After breakfast, he showered and stayed in the basement. When he did come upstairs, he parked himself on the sofa in the family room and looked at his phone. He didn't actively engage with me, Jeff, the girls, or even the dog. He went out Sunday afternoon to run a couple of errands. I tried a gentler approach that day, but he would not give me any information about what had happened earlier in the week. I wanted to believe what he had told me, but I had a feeling in my gut that something worse had happened.

CHAPTER 14

Sam's Writing

Found in Google Docs

*I*t's 9/7/15, 4 a.m. and I can't sleep, and for once I think I have a pretty good handle on why. After some introspection and reading, I'm like 95% sure that I have bipolar disorder. I began to think of this possibility after examining my behavior in the last week, during which I have gone from being incredibly energetic and optimistic to becoming completely hopeless and attempting to OD to being back to where I started two days later. This realization (assuming my self-diagnosis to be true) is jarring, but it explains a great deal of my erratic behavior of the last 19 years. Since I can't sleep anyways, I'll try and list as many instances of this as I can. IDK why but it seems important to me at this moment. The fact that I'm doing this at this hour pretty much proves the fact that I have some elements of hypomania, to say the very least.

Ego fluctuating between extreme self-doubt and self-hatred to severe overconfidence as regarding these factors:

1) Looks: At different points in my life, I have either believed I looked like shit (4/10) or am like a 9/10 and felt that pretty much every girl I passed checked me out to the point of delusion. I would be considered to be good-looking by most.

2) Intelligence: Most of my life I thought I was the shit, intellectually. But recently I have been feeling dumb (thanks Ga Tech!). I think the concept of IQ is bullshit, but mine is probably in the 130's, that is pretty smart, but I'm no genius, although during adolescence I predicted my IQ to be around 150, that I know now to definitely not be true.

3) *Creativity: no need for explanation here. Not very creative of me, I know.*

4) *Taste: I never really considered taste until I got into fashion. At times, I feel that I have an immaculate aesthetic sense. At other times, I feel that I've made horrible decisions in what I was wearing or my choice in room decoration (Why so many rapper posters??) This sometimes results in multiple wardrobe changes per day, that honestly isn't that much of a problem, as I actively enjoy assembling outfits, but I can at times get noided that I look freakish.*

I have severe fluctuations in general mood and outlook on life. I spent the better part of this year significantly depressed only to completely flip flop (and flop and flop) a week ago.

Much of my lack of success in social relationships can be explained by this disorder. During high school, I would rapidly fall into and out of friendships and cliques, at times feeling warmness towards others and at other times complete detachment and disregard. Per consequence of this tendency in conjunction with my more generalized social anxiety, I have few friends and have never been involved in a significant romantic relationship. I can think of several instances where I've snapped at or been incredibly cold to close friends without a sensical reason, such as the time I abruptly drunk drove home from a party, leaving a fuck you message in the group MMS. Hell, the whole getting-dropped-from-Delta-Sig situation can be attributed to the symptoms of this disorder. At parties, I would act grandiose, disconcerted, and downright weird. It also explains how I entirely fell out with a group of guys with whom upon meeting the first time, I felt I could get along exceptionally well with. In general, I think people have a hard time understanding me. I didn't really understand me (in a clinical sense [sorry for the overconfidence of self-diagnosis. I blame the disease]) until an hour ago.

I have a strong tendency to entertain incredibly grand and vain fantasies at length. It happens automatically, like one moment I'll be zoning out in Optics and I'll catch myself fantasizing about winning the Nobel Prize or curing cancer. Sometimes I'll even begin to attach a delusional belief to these visualizations, but logic is sufficient to correct for this (I know I'm not Nobel Laureate material). This love for striving for some fundamental, profound greater good is what drove me to major in physics in the first place, feeling that aerospace engineering was too mundane. Even if this decision was fueled by grandiose delusion (that I don't believe it was), it seems to be the right one so far. I much prefer the administrivia and subject matter of pure science over that of engineering, and I feel it fits my academic strengths much better, even if most would consider it an objectively more difficult path.

However, just as ready to believe that I will do great things, I just as readily believe that it is only a matter of time before I crash, burn, and end up dying alone. And since the latter situation is much more believable than the former, a logical check often does not work here, and I can potentially spiral into depression, that is what happened when I attempted to OD.

I road rage hard at times.

At times, I'll feel the urge to be around others. At other times, I'll feel an equally strong if not greater desire to be alone with my thoughts, that is often the underlying motive behind my sudden and sporadic, albeit uncommon, hostility in unpleasant social situations.

I'm not on any drugs, but I feel high right now. Like I can actually feel the serotonin flowing through my brain (I'm familiar with the feeling from the use of LSD & MDMA).

My ability to sleep varies dramatically. I have bouts of insomnia during mania and lie in bed all day when my depression is severe. Sleep rules everything around me.

Most of the time, I am not entirely wired or depressed, but a confusing and disheartening mix of the two extremes. My thoughts rapid-fire between the two—that is rough, to say the least.

My weight fluctuates between 140 and 165 pounds in accordance to my mental state. I'm pretty fucking hungry right now, but I don't want to be a fat-ass, so I'll hold off.

I'll randomly get the drive to do something productive and positive, like volunteer work or learn a second language, but will flake when it comes down to doing it or otherwise fall out with the idea.

I engage in risk-taking behavior, especially in the form of drug use. If someone passed me a glass dick and offered a hit of crystal, I'm pretty sure I'd take it. Luckily, I'm in a situation where no one is offering me the archetypal "deadly drugs" although I have considered trying low doses of heroin. Furthermore, my friends are pretty reasonable and stick to the standard weed and alcohol with an occasional psychedelic trip. The only substantial drug habit I've had lasted from the latter half of my freshman year until the end of summer, during that I smoked about an eighth of tree per week. That in and of itself is not so bad, but I definitely had an issue with motivation last semester, that was more likely the result of me hating my classes (they were remarkably dull and unrelated to my fields of interest).

I honestly cannot trust myself with money. In the last two years, I have probably spent $2500 on high-end apparel items. When I only had around $600 to my very name, I used $250 of it to impulse buy a pair of Margielas (shout out to the Mr. Porter seasonal sales!). After I bought a pair of semi-designer (whatever you would label an APC X Retrosuperfuture collab) sunglasses, I literally told myself, "I am good on apparel, I need to save money for the school year." But the summer sales kept coming, man... those discounts tho. I had to have muh minimalistic Scandinavian-inspired semi-streetwear (sidewalk-wear? can this be a thing? cause you know it's like next to the street) look for the academic year. And the discounts were good; everything I bought was at least 50% off from retail. I ended up spending another $450 on four items (plus another $93 I dropped on 3 oz of YSL men's cologne). Honestly, the fact that I only did that number is a sign of significant improvement.

I am generally easily scammed as I let go of money with ease. There have been times when I've been at least tempted to go with a dicey business decision for self-destruction's sake.

I also have easily spent that amount or more on drugs since the summer began.

Holy shiiit I just looked at my account balance, and I NEED to stop eating out. I'm just glad that I'm picking up a couple of paychecks tomorrow.

I believe that mania significantly improves my writing ability, as my rapid-fire pattern of thought gives my diction a unique flow. Or maybe my writing sucks and I just have an over-inflated ego. One thing's for sure though, for my writing to be presentable I have to spend a good deal of time cleaning it up. I have found that just writing my thoughts out at the end of a day has great catharsis. Since beginning this document, I've come to accept my condition a great deal more than when I began. It helps me keep things in perspective and grants a degree of emotional clarity.

Things like video games or anything competitive can result in me occasionally having violent outbursts when things go badly. (IDK might just have Sore-Loser Syndrome) A strong example of this was when I gave the finger to the lane judge who disqualified me in county finals. I didn't think; it just happened. That has to be one of the most embarrassing moments of my life. Being aware of bipolar disorder has made me more at peace with it, I think.

I should note that I have never had a proper manic episode, that would result in hospitalization. Wait — shit, I just realized that my recent attempted OD would have probably led to hospitalization had anyone known just how much fucked up I was (35-45 mg Xanax + 4 alcohols consumed within 5 min). Luckily, I seem to have a tolerance to benzos. Otherwise, I would likely be dead. Or not. You can't really OD off benzos alone, and I probably needed significantly more alcohol if I wanted to go out proper. So, I guess I have had a proper moderate-to-severe bipolar episode. But every other time it could be described as hypomania with depression.

I doubted that I displayed elements of paranoia until about a few minutes ago when I realized that my sudden arousal of extreme self-consciousness is pretty much akin to paranoia, as it is a nagging obsession over something that probably isn't true. I'm basically socially anxious because I'm afraid that people think I'm weird...that I guess I am, but not in the way that others actually perceive, to my knowledge.

If I do, in fact, have manic depression, then I am certain that my mom also has this condition, as we share many of these tendencies. It seems likely that I either inherited this disposition (I'm trying to avoid the word "disorder" to stay positive.) from her or picked it up from behavioral adaptation if that's even possible. As soon as I can, I need to confide this in her as well as confess to my need for medical attention (and potentially her need too).

So... what does this mean for me going forward. Well, first off, that I should get an ACTUAL diagnosis and potential treatment from a psychiatrist/clinical psychologist. I was prescribed an SSRI about a month or so ago but never took it. I'm not a big believer in prescription drugs of that nature, as I believe them to be the consequence of a fucked-up medical-legal order that prohibits what has long-term viability in favor of whatever makes money. Additionally, it would block or decrease the effects of my favorite drugs that have helped me cope with myself in the past.

Most people would advise me to lay off the illicit substances, but most people don't know shit about drugs. I will avoid depressants, minus a moderate and socially acceptable level of drinking at the appropriate times, as they tend to induce depressive episodes. Sorry Future and Gucci, there will be no double-cupping for me. :(On a similar note, I've made the switch from bud to wax. As wax has a higher ratio of THC to CBDs, its effects tend to be more cerebral than that of herb (thus resembling more of a stimulant/hallucinogen than a depressant).

I will give micro dosing LSD another go, as it is the sole thing that pulled me up from the crushing depression that dominated this year. With that said, I will err on the side of caution having learned my lesson. A micro-dose is not to be trifled with. Although subtle, if you have a bad trip, you will likely be convinced that it is you thinking those things and not the drug (trust me, it's the drug).

I admit that I had taken a micro-dose (was on the heavy side of threshold @ ~30 mics, thus inducing a light but intense trip instead of stimulation) as a last-ditch effort to turn my day around before attempting suicide. The drug may have negatively influenced my decision-making process in this case. In response to this, it may be considered unwise to continue my relationship with Lucy; however, now having been through the worst of it (can't get any lower than suicide), I have the knowledge to use the drug for good. With acid, the mindset is absolutely everything. If you feel like shit when you take it, you will feel even worse. I find that the best timing to dose is at the beginning of the day, as it offers a fresh start of sorts, that almost invariably ends up in a positive trip or micro-dose.

As far as stimulants go, I will tread on the side of caution as I can definitely see myself ending up dependent on something like cocaine. I will, however, continue to fucks wit tha Molly, as it is pretty much a thrice-yearly miracle drug for those who suffer from anxiety. MDMA has definitely improved my ability to understand others and be confident in a social setting in addition to just bettering my relationships with those whom I roll around. (<–beautiful unintentional double-entendre :)

But other than that, shit hasn't really changed. My brain's still the same; I just have a new word to attribute all my problems to (jokes). In the past, I've blamed my failings on stuff like low self-esteem and an external locus of self-control, but I now see that that was only half the truth. I gotta be straight with myself, despite my problems, I definitely haven't done that badly at life, that depression would have me oft believe. At the end of the day, I'm studying a subject I'm good at and enjoy at a great school. I'm an attractive upper-middle-class American (pretty much cheating at life LMAO), I have awesome people in my life who have stuck by me through the thick of it, and to top it all off, I have good taste in clothes! I just have a bit of a mood disorder but who the fuck doesn't these days?

CHAPTER 15

A Crushing Truth and Seeking Help

In bed and half-awake, a ray of sun shining through the window hit my closed eye. I blinked both eyes open and groggily remembered that it was Labor Day. I got out of bed and stripped the sheets to wash them. On my way downstairs, I paused on the catwalk that overlooks our two-story family room. What I saw made me hesitate. Jeff and Sam were on the sofa, talking—not just talking, but having a quiet, focused conversation. Their heads were bent toward one another, and Jeff cupped his coffee mug in both hands. Sam's thick brown hair was uncombed, and he was wearing one of my old 10K race shirts that I store in the basement. What was going on? And why would he get into my race shirts? I descended the stairs.

"What's going on?" I asked as I entered the family room.

"Sam has been telling me that he's pretty sure he has bipolar disorder," Jeff responded.

I gave Jeff a concerned, quizzical look and sat next to Sam. Jeff moved over to the armchair next to Sam's end of the couch.

"Sam, I have known you for all of your nineteen years, and I have never witnessed you in any state of mania," I declared, feeling my own anxiety heightening.

He quickly refuted that by citing a couple of cases where he had acted impulsively. He continued speaking in a rapid-fire manner, jumping topics, seeming indeed *manic*. I didn't ask if he was high, but I wondered.

"Mom, you and I are so alike. I think you might also be bipolar." In saying this, he seemed sincere, like he really wanted to help me. I was both touched and unnerved by his insistence.

"Sam, I am not bipolar. I have had mild to moderate depression since my early teens, though," I replied. My depression was something I'd never discussed with my three children. I felt a little vulnerable doing so now, but I also knew it was imperative that I share with him my experience as a point of reference.

"Really? What meds have you tried? Have you ever seen a therapist? Does therapy work?" He jumped breathlessly from one question to the next. He asked me again if I was sure I wasn't bipolar. "I think you and I both are," he said. "You need to consider the chance that you are. I want to get help for my bipolar condition so that I can do better at life."

I looked over at Jeff, who was nodding at Sam. This was a typical response from Jeff; he has always hated confrontation.

I detailed my limited history with psychotherapy (my last experience had been in 2007 and had started as marital counseling) and antidepressants (Wellbutrin and Lexapro prescribed by my general practitioner). I told Sam that running and exercise, in addition to conventional therapy options, had always been mood enhancers for me.

"How do you do that—still feel motivated to exercise on a regular basis?" he asked.

"Having a friend to work out with helps. That keeps me accountable. If you set a regular routine of going with a friend at a set time, it would probably help." Sam seemed to consider this, and I felt a moment of hope.

For almost an hour, Jeff and I tried to keep up with what Sam was saying. Maggie and Claire were in their rooms, sleeping in on a holiday weekend morning. Listening to Sam was both troubling and exhausting. My mind whirled with a combination of wanting to help him and wanting him to just stop talking and acting this way. This wasn't Sam. He had never acted like this with us before. We assured him he had options, we would get him treatment, and he could take a break from school if needed.

After the conversation, Sam went into the basement to shower. Jeff and I talked about what we should do. We were both dumbfounded at Sam's hyperintensity and scared of what it meant. I felt helpless not knowing where to start with our intervention. For the short term, we settled on Jeff taking Sam kayaking, just the two of them, to attempt to get more information about how Sam had arrived at his self-diagnosis.

When he came back upstairs after showering, he seemed more like our Sam. He had showered and shaved and put on fresh clothes—his own this time. He and Jeff loaded the kayaks in the back of our minivan and left. I had promised Maggie and Claire our own outing for Labor Day. I took them to Old Navy and Target to shop for school clothes and supplies, and after, the three of us went to see *Inside Out*. My thoughts rarely strayed from Sam that afternoon.

By the time the girls and I came home, it was late afternoon. Jeff was in the kitchen and Sam had gone out to run an errand. The girls went upstairs to their rooms.

"Did Sam tell you any more about what's going on?" I asked Jeff. I was hoping for a reassuring answer, something to ease my worry.

"Yeah, but he asked that I not tell you until he's back at school."

I insisted Jeff tell me.

He did. It was the moment when my life changed forever.

"Sam tried to kill himself last week."

I braced myself on the back of a kitchen chair, then lost my grip and slid to the floor. I took huge gulps of air that came back out as throaty sobs. Jeff didn't want the girls to know about Sam's attempt; he grabbed hold of me and led me upstairs to our bedroom and shut the door.

I lay on our still-unmade bed, sobbing with such ferocity that I was too exhausted to even wipe the tears and snot from my face. Jeff went into the bathroom and came back with a roll of toilet paper. Although sympathetic, he seemed mostly concerned that the kids would hear me crying. I choked out some questions but could scarcely take in even the limited information he gave me. Jeff lay beside me. As a mother, this was the one scenario I had never allowed myself to envision. Under no circumstances could I have ever allowed my mind drift to the possible death of one of my children. Even further, to think that one of my kids would take his or her own life felt the worst kind of hell, the one thing I was certain would kill me, too.

AN HOUR LATER, I rinsed my face and brushed my hair, trying to pull myself together. I went to sit in our family room. Soon after, Sam came home from his errands. He walked slowly into the kitchen from the garage, glancing over at me.

I patted the sofa seat next to me. "Will you sit with me?" I asked.

He did, clearly dreading what was to come.

I told him his dad had told me. Sam didn't seem surprised. He said he'd been depressed all summer. He had hoped that the beginning of his second year at Georgia Tech would be better, but in a few short days, he had lost all motivation. He told me that he had had suicidal thoughts for at least the last five years. Hearing this, I felt small and impotent. If this had been going on for so long, what had I been doing? Why wasn't I paying attention?

To attempt suicide, Sam told me he taken fifty milligrams of Xanax and several shots of whiskey. As far as I knew, Sam did not have a prescription for Xanax. I imagined that he had either bought it off the street or the dark web. Researching this later, I found that a normally prescribed dose of the drug is no more than four milligrams daily, meaning that Sam had taken twelve-and-a-half times a recommended amount. As I listened, Sam told me how the mixture had left him completely out of it for a full day and a half. He had no memory of that time, but it was during that episode that he'd cracked his phone and gotten the scrapes on his face and hands. He also told me that he had vomited—a lot.

Sam went on to tell me that after he came to, he told his roommates about the attempt. One of them said to him, "Sam, you either tell your parents about this or I will." That was why he had called Jeff on Saturday morning requesting a ride home. It had taken him until Monday afternoon to tell Jeff about the attempted suicide.

The truth crushed me. I wondered how I could not have seen. I had tricked myself into believing a kid who was so accomplished and still succeeding could not be severely depressed. In my mind, depression and especially suicidal thoughts rendered one unable to function well. I questioned, too, whether I should have intervened more forcefully in his weed use.

Sam and I talked quietly for a while. My heart was full of pain. I could not lose him. I loved him at that moment as much as I ever had. At some point, I grabbed his hands and looked into his eyes. "Sam, you might as well kill me first, because this is something I would never be able to survive."

He looked doubtful. I could tell he didn't believe me, but I repeated the statement. I elicited a promise from him that he would never do this to himself and to us. I told him that he would not only be ending his life but forever destroying the lives of his family. I knew how much Sam cared about his family, and I thought that, maybe, if he didn't want to stay alive for himself, he'd at least stay alive for us long enough to get help.

For some reason, my mind turned to the idea of a suicide note. I asked Sam if he had written one.

"Yeah, a half-ass one."

My head was spinning. Rather than ask what he'd written in his note, I asked, "Sam, do you realize how lucky we are that you survived the overdose?"

"Well, you know, drug overdoses are a successful means of suicide only ten percent of the time."

"Maybe that's so," I told him. "But what about the people who end up clinically alive but in a vegetative state?"

I told Sam I didn't want him to go back to school until we found him help.

But Sam was wholly resistant to this idea. "I'm fine, and I can't afford to take any time off," he said. "Anyway, since I told my roommates, they'll keep an eye on me." Sam might have acknowledged his need for help, but it was clear he was resistant to the idea of taking time off. He had created his four-year college plan, and I believe he felt deeply driven to stick to it. Perhaps he also hadn't wanted to admit that our world had permanently shifted.

I told him that wasn't enough. "You are a danger to yourself. I think the drugs you are using are contributing to your despondence."

I found myself begging Sam to stay home so we could find the best care for him. Jeff took a different tactic. He believed Sam when he said this would never happen again and thought it was okay for him to return to school. I was frustrated by Jeff's position and thought it was an example of his sometimes-questionable optimism, his propensity for always looking at the world through rose-colored glasses. But his reaction was also on some level understandable; heretofore, we had never faced anything this scary.

DURING DINNER THAT evening, Sam told me he had a loss of appetite and hadn't slept since coming out of the OD. Since our conversation that afternoon, I'd started noticing cognitive lapses in him. He seemed unable to process or answer even simple questions. When we had sat down for dinner, he had appeared to not know how to put his napkin in his lap—or, more accurately, what the purpose of the napkin was. I wasn't sure if it was the lack of sleep, if he was already using again, or if he had damaged his brain during the overdose.

I was still firm in not wanting Sam to return to Tech, but he said that after the attempt, he would never do anything like that again. He claimed that, in fact, he felt energy and motivation to get back to school and buckle down. Those were his words, but his body language told a different story. He moved lethargically and purpose-lessly about the house throughout the afternoon and evening.

Sam was scheduled to go back to Tech that evening, to start classes the next day. I continued to plead that he not return, but Sam seemed unlikely to change his point of view willingly and Jeff remained on his side. He said it felt like Sam regretted the action and would be okay. I was fighting them both, and I had no real idea of what Sam would do with his time if he acquiesced and didn't go back to school. I felt helpless and confused.

I let Sam go back to school with caveats. The next morning, I would call to find a psychiatrist either through the school or privately, and Sam had to commit to seeing both a psychiatrist and a psychologist on a regular basis until we could obtain a firm diagnosis and get him appropriately medicated. Sam agreed. I said I would make inquiries at Tech to find out what help their mental health center could provide.

Sam went back to Tech that evening. I felt angry with Jeff because he hadn't backed me up, and I told him so. In the past, Jeff had expressed that he thought I overreacted to situations regarding our kids. He has always been the type to think everything is going to work out in the end. I should have held my ground. I didn't. My advice to anyone who will listen is to follow your gut. Especially as a mother, you pick up on the vibrations of your offspring. The pull to want to minimize things—to just reset everything to normal—is strong. Listen to those vibrations; hold your son or daughter in your arms. Do not be swayed by anyone who says your instincts are wrong.

TUESDAY MORNING, NOT knowing where else to turn, I called our pediatrician to ask for her advice. Sam had last seen her the year before, for his 18-year-old checkup. She recommended getting Sam to a psychiatric hospital for an evaluation and gave me the names of three Atlanta-area mental health hospitals.

I started calling the hospitals. The intake person I spoke with at the first hospital seemed unconcerned and lackadaisical. I immediately dismissed it as a possibility. The second one, Lakeview Hospital, recommended bringing Sam in for an evaluation as soon as possible. We did not need an appointment. I didn't call the third one.

I phoned Sam and told him we were coming to school to get

him and take him to the hospital for a mental evaluation. He wasn't happy, but he agreed. The three of us—me, Sam, and Jeff—made the drive from the Georgia Tech campus to Lakeview that morning.

The hospital was located in a large technology park just twelve miles from home, twenty miles from campus but still in metro Atlanta. It was an unassuming structure; the exterior looked more like an office building than a hospital. Inside, the lobby was stark: institutional vinyl flooring, fluorescent lighting, and metal-and-black-plastic chairs lined up along one wall. Planters of plastic greenery flanked the front desk. I walked over to a large window on a wall opposite the front door. Just outside was a small manmade lake. *Ah, hence Lakeview,* I thought.

We waited two-and-a-half hours for Sam to be seen. Apparently, a lot of people overdose on Labor Day weekend. Ambulances kept arriving, and the hospital was chaotic. Eventually, only Sam and a twentysomething woman were left waiting to be seen. Sam was next in line, but when the nurse called his name, he pointed toward the young woman and said they should see her first because she seemed to be worse off. In truth, she did look like she was in both physical pain and mental anguish. She said she was experiencing sharp pain around one of her kidneys. That might very well have been true, but it was also clear she was having some type of psychotic episode.

The girl thanked Sam and followed the nurse. My patience worn thin, anxious for him to be seen by the evaluator, I let out an aggravated sigh and gave Sam a frustrated look.

"Mom, stop being so passive-aggressive," he said.

I didn't reply.

Finally, Sam was called back. Jeff and I remained in the waiting room. We were not asked to participate in the evaluation. After 45 minutes, Sam emerged and said the recommendation from the evaluator was for him to either start an outpatient program that would have him at the hospital from 8:00 a.m. until 5:00 p.m. Monday through Saturday for a minimum of two weeks, or to immediately get an appointment with the Georgia Tech counseling department.

Neither Jeff nor I asked if we could speak with the evaluator. Now, I have no idea why we didn't.

"Did the evaluator think you were well enough to go back to school? She didn't recommend inpatient hospitalization?" I asked.

Sam muttered something in the negative.

I broached the subject of him taking some time off from Tech to complete the outpatient program, but he immediately rejected the idea. He promised he'd get to Georgia Tech's Stamps Health Center's mental health offices that day, or first thing in the morning. He assured us he was feeling okay.

I wanted him to be okay. I wanted this to be the one-off he said it was. I felt helpless both because Sam was over 18, and therefore technically allowed to make his own decisions, and because I didn't know where else to turn for help. Jeff and I agreed he could go back to campus. Jeff took him back to school around 3:00 that afternoon.

Before he left, I made Sam promise that he would go to the Stamps Center as soon as he got to campus to get started on a treatment plan. When I called him that evening, he said it had been too late to go to Stamps after he'd gone to his lab. I told him, "Sam, first thing in the morning, go there. Do not go to class." Then I asked how he was feeling.

"I'm down, but not out," was his reply.

He seemed a little blurred, and I felt like he'd either been drinking or using. Or maybe he was just exhausted. Either way, his sentence unnerved me.

WEDNESDAY MORNING, I called Sam to make sure he had made it over to Stamps. He didn't answer. I texted him at 10:00 a.m. and asked him to give me a call, please. Sometime later, he called and said the delay in getting back to me was because he was on the campus bus, adding that he had had to put his phone in airplane mode because his data had been skyrocketing for no reason. He told me he would go to Stamps after his next class. In the late afternoon, Sam called and said he had walked all the way to the Stamps Center only to find out that if he wanted to book an appointment with a counselor, he first had to participate in a phone interview. He was told the first available phone appointment would be Friday.

Frustrated, I called Lakeview. After speaking with the receptionist, I was transferred to Carmen, the intake counselor Sam had seen. She told me that she had not wanted to release him, but because he was not a minor, she hadn't had a choice. Contrary to what Sam had told us, she had in fact recommended inpatient hospitalization, as that would be the most efficient avenue for getting him the right dosages of the right medications. My stomach dropped.

Inpatient hospitalization would also allow for daily sessions with a psychiatrist and a psychologist and ongoing group and individual therapy, she said. Trying to get adequate treatment outside of a hospital takes much longer, and we would likely wait at least two weeks to get an appointment with a psychiatrist. The trial and error to find the best medications for Sam would therefore also be that much more drawn-out. When I told Carmen that Sam had said he could not get help from the university's mental health care office until he had a phone appointment, she said she would call them.

Soon after, Carmen called back. She had made headway with the counseling center at Tech and said Sam should go there now and just walk in; they were expecting him. I immediately called Sam and told him he had to go there now or I would drive to campus and escort him. Sam repeated what they had said to him that morning about the process of seeing someone. Feeling frustrated with both Sam and the system, I spoke firmly to him. I told him he needed to go there right now, give Carmen's name, ask for Dr. Bowers, and fill out the registration form at the front desk, and he would be seen. Sam said he would go after a lab, but his tone suggested he was noncommittal at best. In the end, he didn't go.

Later, I found a text exchange sent from Sam to a friend that began, "L on deck." L meant LSD. The text was sent at 6:20 p.m., after our phone conversation and his lab. Sam was once again self-medicating.

Finally, on Thursday, Sam kept his promise and saw Dr.

Bowers at Stamps Mental Health Center. Dr. Bowers called me while Sam was in the office with him. He said that obviously Sam had done a good bit of reading and research into his condition and had diagnosed himself as having bipolar disorder. Although he could not make a diagnosis yet, Dr. Bowers strongly recommended that he escort Sam to the dean's office so that Sam could withdraw from Tech for the semester. The doctor said it was essential that Sam focus his full concentration on getting well. He noted that the withdrawal would be listed as a medical leave of absence and that Sam would not be penalized in any way regarding grades, scholarships, or anything else. It was gratifying, and something of a relief, that the doctor was taking Sam's suicide attempt and depression as seriously as I was. But I also felt fear of what the next steps would be.

When I asked Dr. Bowers about hospitals, he suggested taking Sam to Ridgeview Institute, located northwest of Atlanta in Smyrna, Georgia. Dr. Bowers put Sam on the phone. I tried to sound encouraging. "Sam, now we have a plan. Go with Dr. Bowers to the dean's office and withdraw, then go to your dorm and pack an overnight bag. I'm on my way to pick you up."

Solemnly, he agreed. I didn't ask but wondered how Sam felt about the conversation with Dr. Bowers and the new plan of action.

I called Jeff and told him to meet us at Ridgeview. Then I drove into Atlanta and waited for Sam outside his campus apartment building. I'm not sure what I expected his mood to be, but because he'd never been combative with me before, what ensued shocked me.

When Sam walked out of the campus apartment building toward my car, I could tell from his body language that he was furious with me. He slung his overnight bag into the back seat and got into the front seat, slamming the door.

"How are you feeling?" I asked.

"How would you feel?" he demanded. "Honestly, you are the one who needs help."

I tried to pacify him, but he would have none of it. He continued his angry rant, going as far as to say that Maggie and Claire should not live with me until I got psychological help. I was rattled by his sharpness of tone and his obvious fury with me. When I missed a turn to get to the hospital, he snapped at me.

Jeff was already there when we got to Ridgeview. We checked Sam in, and all three of us sat in the waiting room. Sam was jittery, not able to sit still—completely different from his demeanor only a few days before in the waiting room at Lakeview, when he had offered to give the young woman his spot. He continued to focus all his energy and attention on me, claiming that he was psychologically sound and I was the one who needed to get help. Trying to appease him, I promised I would.

"Don't say that unless you really mean it," he spat.

On the verge of losing it in the face of his fury, I walked outside, telling Jeff to text me when Sam was called back. The day was overcast and drizzly, fitting my mood. I sat in my car and allowed myself to cry. I had found my bottom, or at least I thought I had. A person I had loved and treasured throughout his entire life had just rejected me in every way possible. He also seemed hellbent on rejecting himself.

I didn't wait for Jeff's text. After thirty minutes, I went back in, choosing a seat apart from Jeff and Sam. Soon afterward, Sam was called in for the evaluation. Jeff and I remained in the waiting room. I'm not sure how much time elapsed before the evaluator came out to report on Sam. She said he was very animated and talkative and invited us back to her office.

Apart from our conversation three days earlier, I had never seen Sam in any type of manic state. But he was then. Jeff and I sat with him in the evaluation room and listened as the evaluator recommended hospitalization into their psychiatric wing, rather than the substance abuse wing. I could scarcely take in her words.

She asked Sam if he would share all hospital information and records with his parents. He said he would share with his dad, but he added, "Because my mom is the primary reason I'm here, I don't think I want her to have access." The evaluator turned her head from Sam to look at me, and I felt like she was judging me as some unfit mom. Maybe that was what I was. I felt humiliated. I meekly said that was his choice.

Once again, Sam turned his anger on me. He said that most of his existence, he had been living with me raging and screaming. Because I marginalized his dad, he had not grown up respecting or appreciating his dad as he should. I was the reason, he said, for his fear of being rejected by girls and for his incompetent social state. I forced him to do things he did not want to do, like swimming. He said he felt he could never meet my high expectations. "You destroy all who are around you," he declared, looking at me with clear anger on his face.

His words hit me like physical blows, and with each one, I retreated farther into the corner of the green vinyl sofa where I sat. I curled my legs underneath me and hunched my shoulders and my arms into my body, as though I could physically protect myself from my son's hatred. I wanted to disappear. He eventually agreed to me having access to his medical records, because I would "badger Dad" until I got the information anyway.

Sam could not focus enough to answer the questions on the admission form he had to fill out. Jeff sat beside him, asking him the list of questions and filling in the answers for him. Sam made a dig at me at every opportunity. When a question about sexuality and relationships came up, Sam responded that living in a household where his mom was always disparaging his dad had caused him to have social anxiety around girls. I felt a mix of guilt and defensiveness. Was every problem he'd experienced in life my fault?

He continued, "Mom doesn't want me to have a relationship with anyone but her."

"Sam, you know that isn't true," I whispered. I'm not sure he heard me.

At 10:00 p.m., Sam was still in the admissions process. Because Jeff and I had come in two cars, I told them I would go home to be with the girls. I tentatively walked over to Sam, kissed his cheekbone, and softly said that I loved him.

"I love you, too," he said with urgency. "I just need you to get well." He hugged me. I offered to take his watch and wallet home with me, and he handed both items over.

I WILL NEVER forget that ride home. Going around I-285 and then north on I-85, I kept willing myself to crash into a concrete barrier and die. I did not want to harm anyone else, but my pain and distress made me think that Jeff, Sam, and the girls would be better off without me. I felt singularly responsible for Sam's depression and suicide attempt. In my despair, I thought a quick death would both alleviate my pain and save Sam.

Instead, I completed the drive home. My conscious mind told me that I could not do that to my husband, children, or parents; my unconscious mind knew that my innate sense of self-preservation would not allow me. I hated myself more than I ever had, more even than I had in my deepest adolescent depressive state.

When I got home, Maggie and Claire were in the family room, sitting together and obviously troubled. They stood and walked over to me as I came into the house, their sweet, beautiful faces scrunched in concern. The television was on, but at a low volume. I told them that Jeff was with Sam. I said Sam was very sad and was in a hospital to get better. I never mentioned the suicide attempt because I thought that they were too young to bear that. I assured them that Sam would be okay and would be taking a break from Tech and coming home for a while. They nodded but did not ask any questions. I wondered if they were afraid of the answers. With tears welling up in their eyes, they told me goodnight and went to their rooms.

As soon as they went to bed, I went upstairs and locked myself in my bathroom. I wailed and begged, "God, help my son. Take away his despair. Please spare him. Take me first." Kneeling on the cold tile, I was in such a state that when I raised my head, I inadvertently hit my eyebrow on the sharp edge of the tile surrounding the tub. As head wounds do, the cut bled profusely.

In another hour or so, Jeff arrived and asked if he should take me to the emergency room for stitches.

"Of course not," I said. "Who cares what happens to me?"

CHAPTER 16

Sam's Writing

Written during His Stay at Ridgeview Institute

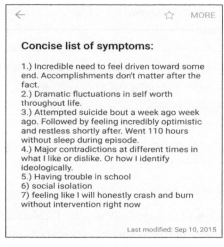

From Sam's phone, written while waiting for admission

9/10/15: Asides from weed (only as needed or appropriate—this is important), I should stay off drugs and on meds and in counseling. I realize as well that I feel the need to always be striving for a goal; the accomplishments seem to be less important. So, I should allow myself to progress slowly.

9/11/15: I have discovered, thanks to treatment methods, that I have an exceptionally narcissistic personality. And it really does suck. It makes me think way more of myself than is reasonable. I'm beginning to notice some triggers that cause irrational behavior that cause me to act inappropriately, creating isolation between myself and others. Some ways I can improve:

- Not overthink about triggers—that sets them off
- Come to terms with failure
- Don't understate my negative qualities
- Don't use so many positive or negative adverbs, as it connotes being condescending
- Don't over-analyze why I do the things I do
- Don't be too hard on myself when I fail expectations
- Admit faults
- Don't freak out that my condition is worse than it is
- Even if I am "stable," I should stay here and go with the flow and try not to figure everything out when doing so
- Admitting fault is hard
- Don't get paranoid

It's impressive how this works.

9/12/15: Kinda want a cigarette right now, but I'm also wholly averted to them at the moment. I'm feeling better emotionally; it feels good to come to terms with myself, but I'm still not getting much sleep and have almost no appetite. But at least I am making myself eat. I'm definitely adjusting to this place; I felt extremely disoriented coming in. My heart rate and blood pressure have already decreased significantly from when I was first screened at the hospital. The future is incredibly uncertain, but I'm still optimistic.

I think part of my ability to chill is because of the Lexapro. Also, I definitely have a disordered way of eating and have had consistently little appetite since the OD.

9/15/15: I am aware now that during the first couple of days I was here, I had absolutely no touch with reality, but since starting the mood stabilizer and actually getting some sleep, I feel much more level-headed, *to say the least. Since I am pretty much stabilized, it's time that I make an aftercare plan to discuss with my doctor. Here are some things I will do upon being discharged:*

- *Regularly see psychiatrist and counselor*
- *Avoid all illicit or otherwise psychoactive substances and those who would pressure me into doing such substances*
- *Continue to regularly participate in AA meetings*
- *Consistently take meds as prescribed, and if I ever feel that I can be off the meds, then it means the meds are working and that I should continue taking them*
- *Go back to work at my low-stress job to give myself some structure*
- *Make time to learn something or improve a skill. I still have the textbooks from the classes I had to withdraw from and teaching myself that material would be beneficial for when I return to school. Namely, Honors Physics II. I would also like to practice French so that I can do a study abroad program next summer*
- *Utilize a calendar program to schedule these things and hold myself accountable*
- *Get an appropriate amount of exercise daily. I'll alternate running with weight training*
- *Have a creative outlet. Right now, I'd like to make beats, but I should allow myself to be spontaneous and have no expectations*
- *Make time to read*
- *Volunteer at charitable organizations such as the local animal shelter*
- *Visit my friends at their colleges during weekends I'm not working*
- *Apply for scholarships for people with bipolar disorder*

CHAPTER 17

Visitation Day

Saturday, 9/12/15

Dear Sam,

I'm not going to deny what you said to and about me Thursday when you were admitted to the hospital. I've been thinking it over, and I won't try to defend myself.

I am a control freak and nearly impossible to live with. I'm sorry for the way I have treated your dad. He is a good man, and he deserves better.

I wish I had been a better mother. I have made mistakes daily, and you and your sisters are the innocent victims. But, although I wish my actions were better, I could never have loved you, Maggie, and Claire any more than I did and do.

When I want to make myself feel better, I have a very clear image of you in the Nashville airport when you were three. I had just arrived in Nashville from being in Paris, and you had stayed with Mom Mary and Pop. As we walked to baggage claim (pre-9/11 you could meet people at the gates), you took my hand and impulsively kissed it over and over and held it to your sweet face. That's the Sam I know, the one with a huge heart for animals, the elderly, the unfortunate, and the mistake-ridden mother.

I am heartbroken that you felt in such a hopeless situation that the only way out was to kill yourself. I feel like I've been in a nightmare since Monday, and I cannot wake myself up.

No matter what you decide to do with your life—and it has only begun—Dad and I will love you and support you. Do what you want with your education and career. GT may not be the best place for you, and we will back your decision for a change: emotionally, financially, and any other way needed. It's your life, Kiddo.

I am making a pledge to you that I am going to get help with controlling my anger. I'm looking into cognitive therapy for impulse control. I acknowledge that my constant state of fury has affected all of you. I wish I could start over. But since I can't, I will start doing better, today. I promise.

Love, Mom

I wrote Sam this letter while he was hospitalized at Ridgeview. I wrote it before the Saturday visitation time, which was to be from 2:30 to 3:30, the only hour we would be able to see Sam during his hospitalization.

In the six days Sam was in the hospital, he rarely took our calls or returned them. There was only one common phone for the patients to use—no cell phones allowed. On the two times he did speak with us, he kept the conversations brief. We received most of our information through communication from Sam's caseworker, Norma. She felt like an important lifeline for us—our source of connection to and information about Sam. When I talked with her, she was sincere and sympathetic. She told me that Sam was doing better and was meeting regularly with both a psychiatrist and a psychologist and attending all the group sessions.

When the visitation day arrived, Sam had been hospitalized for three days, but it seemed much longer. Anxious to see him, we arrived at the hospital over an hour before the scheduled visitation. As instructed, we left our cell phones in the car and did not take them into the hospital building.

Jeff and I held hands and approached the automatic front doors. It was a mid-September morning, and the first hint of fall was in the air. I wore a casual dress and low-heeled sandals. Jeff wore jeans and a button-down shirt.

The lobby was well-lit, with natural light streaming through two-story windows. The furniture in the room had the clean, straight lines of modern design. I felt an appreciation for the brightness of the sunlight. It was the same lobby that we had been in when Sam had been admitted on Thursday, but the weather had been gloomy that day, and I had been too despondent to really notice my surroundings. Now the clean, warm light gave me a measure of hope.

When I approached the front desk, the receptionist informed me that it was not quite time for visitation and we should wait in the lobby. Then she added, "I've been working here ten years, and you are the first person I've ever seen come to visitation in a dress." I half-smiled. How exactly does one know what to wear to visit a child in a mental institution for the first time?

Other people arrived—mostly midlife adults who mirrored Jeff and me with their anxious looks and somber, whispered conversation. The hour passed slowly. My heart raced for almost all of it. Finally, a hospital official addressed the waiting room. For the first part of visitation, he said, we would be in a general session with a speaker. After this, we would have a short time alone with our patient. We were asked to follow a gentleman into the meeting space. Before being allowed to enter, we had to go through a security detection system, and I had my purse checked. I asked the security guard if we would be allowed to give our son letters. Maggie, Claire, and I had all written to Sam. He replied that that was fine but that he had to open the envelopes first. I handed the three letters to him.

Entering the meeting space felt like entering a classroom on parent night. The surroundings were sterile—straight-backed chairs arranged both in rows and along the perimeter of the room and a single lectern placed at the front. I scanned the room. The patients were mostly adults, ranging in age from perhaps 18 to 50. There was one patient who looked to be no more than 14 or 15 sitting between her parents. I couldn't help but notice how she had her arms wrapped around her father, ignoring her mother.

I spotted Sam's back, his broad swimmer's shoulders atop his otherwise narrow frame. He had on chinos, a white t-shirt, and white Nikes. We walked over to him, and he was tearful as he stood up and hugged us hard. He said he'd been afraid we hadn't remembered visitation day. "I've really missed you guys," he said with a small smile. He looked a little haggard, as he hadn't been allowed to shave and seemed to have lost more weight. Jeff and I sat on either side of him. Sam turned in his chair to face me and said, "I said things to you when I was admitted that I really didn't mean."

I told him it was all okay, that I wanted him to worry more about getting well than about offending me. I told him that I would not desert him, ever. While we sat through a group presentation on how family members could help their patients, I rubbed Sam's back continuously with my right hand. Even with his perfect posture, his shoulder blades jutted out. After a couple of minutes, he asked me to stop. I jerked my hand away and apologized. Minutes later, Jeff grabbed Sam's knee and gave him an affectionate little shake. "No," I said. "He doesn't want to be touched."

Sam said, "I don't mind being touched, but, Mom, you were rubbing my back compulsively."

I had been rubbing his back over and over in a circular motion, and if I could have, I would have drawn him closer to me and held him for the entirety of the meeting. I apologized again, and Sam said not to worry about it. The tie between us felt achingly tenuous, and I was afraid to say or do anything wrong.

After the group session, we were allowed time with Sam alone. We were not permitted into the residential hall, and so instead, we dragged three chairs together in the meeting room in a makeshift seating arrangement. I gave him the letters, and he opened them there. After he read mine, he thanked me. He teared up at all three letters.

Sam appeared sad and apologetic. More than once, he told us he was sorry that he had hurt us. He filled us in on the last three days. He told Jeff and me that the first night there, he had been on suicide watch, which essentially meant he had been strapped to a gurney in a brightly lit hallway all night. An image flashed to mind, one of Sam lying on a hospital bed with perhaps some version of a straitjacket on and unable to sleep. I felt sick.

On his second day, he had been put into a dorm room with an older man, a sweet guy with schizophrenia, Sam said. Sam told us that during his three days at Ridgeview, his mind had jumped from feeling he might also be schizophrenic to feeling like he was the sanest one in the building. Rather than weighing in on what we thought, we told him that we would manage—whatever the diagnosis. Jeff and I had determined on the ride over that we would only be supportive of what Sam had to say.

When it was time to leave, we hugged and kissed him. The visitation time was over, and we would be unable to see him again until the following Saturday, unless he was released before then. Sam behaved as though he was sad to see us leave, and I was again filled with that now-familiar mixture of sadness and guilt. For me, the hug ended too soon. I wanted to hold him longer.

When we got back into our car, I saw I had a missed call and voicemail from an unknown number. It was Sam. He had left it while we had been in the waiting area before visitation hours had begun.

"Hey, it's Sam. I'm calling from the, you know, um, institution's landline. Are you guys coming to visitation hours? They're, like, in about an hour. If you'll just call me back on this number, and I'll wait by the phone to get your call. If you can, just let me know for sure. And, hopefully, I will see you soon."

Listening to the message in the car, I began to cry. How vulnerable he sounded! How heartbreaking that he had wondered whether we would visit. He almost stuttered over the word "institution." Imagining his uncertainty waiting for my return call that hadn't come gave me a physical ache.

We returned home, and I spent the rest of the weekend wandering from room to room, wringing my hands, praying hard, and accomplishing nothing.

CHAPTER 18

Home from the Hospital

Monday morning came, and I tried to work. I had trouble concentrating, but at least work offered a distraction. Around 12:30 p.m., Sam called.

"Mom, I'm feeling much better." His tone was eager. I hoped that this was because he was doing better and not because he was merely trying to convince me that he was ready to come home.

"That's great. Do you know when they might release you?" When Sam had been admitted, the evaluator had been vague about the length of hospitalization. She had said it could be from a week to a month, depending on the psychiatrists' recommendation.

"That's just it—I saw a different psychiatrist today. He was dismissive about releasing me from inpatient to an outpatient program. He said I wasn't ready."

Sam said this doctor had also upped his meds, specifically for a mood stabilizer. He really wanted to get out of the hospital, and my heart strained to make him happy. I told him I had called Norma that morning and left a message, but she hadn't returned my call, yet.

"I'll try again after we get off the phone," I told him.

Sam said one improvement was that he was finally allowed to shave, but only in the cafeteria while someone watched him.

I made two calls after I hung up with Sam. The first was a second phone call to Norma. She wasn't in the office that day, and the call was forwarded to a caseworker who was covering for her. She told me that there had not yet been a decision to discharge Sam. She said that was up to the psychiatrist. When he was released, they would have a family discharge planning session with us before he left the hospital campus. My second call was to the psychiatrist. At this point, we still did not have a diagnosis of Sam's condition. The doctor was not available, and I had to leave a message.

AT NOON THE next day, Sam called Jeff at work, saying he would be released that day. "Please hurry," Sam urged Jeff. "If we're not through with the discharge process before five, I'll have to stay here another night." Jeff called me and picked me up, and together, we rushed to the hospital.

We were soon sitting in front of Norma. I looked at her carefully put-together business suit and felt reassured of her competence. I was grateful to have Sam finally in good hands. Norma listed off information about an aftercare plan, telling us that Sam's release was contingent upon beginning an outpatient program the next day at 9:00 a.m. The doctors wanted him to join the Partial Hospitalization Program (PHP) at Ridgeview, but because the outpatient program ran from 9:00 to 5:00, when traffic from Suwanee to Smyrna, where Ridgeview is located, was at its worst, we elected for Sam to participate in the PHP at Summit Ridge Hospital in Lawrenceville. We were assured that the two hospitals would share information and that Summit Ridge would carefully monitor his condition over the undetermined number of weeks he was required to attend.

I asked Norma for Sam's diagnosis. (Sam was not yet in the room with us.) She said that the two psychiatrists he had seen at the hospital had ruled out bipolar disorder. The doctors had determined that Sam suffered from depression along with a substance-induced mood disorder. She further added that Sam had entered the hospital under a drug-induced psychosis. Strangely, I felt a little relieved to hear this, and I wondered if his verbal attack on me might have been partially due to the drugs. I also thought that depression was a better diagnosis than bipolar disorder, but what did I know?

Moments later, Sam joined us for the discharge meeting. He seemed relieved to be going home and happy to see us. This was short-lived. When Sam learned of his diagnosis, he became angry. He had been convinced that he had bipolar disorder and that treatment for that would be the answer to becoming an improved version of himself. He vehemently rejected that he had been under a drug-induced psychosis when admitted. He said he had smoked a little marijuana that morning but done nothing else. He was released with prescriptions for Lexapro, Abilify, Seroquel, and Trileptal.

We gathered Sam's things and got into the car. I sat in the back seat, leaving the front seat for him. He was sullen and quiet, although his anger somewhat dissipated during the drive home.

At the house, his sisters greeted him with big hugs. He looked pale and exhausted and soon went to bed. I cannot remember whether we all ate dinner together, but after dinner, I asked Sam if he would return to his old room upstairs. My thought was that we could keep an eye on him better if he were upstairs, and he would be forced to interact with us more. The basement, on the other hand, provided him with his own bedroom, bathroom, and media area. All that would potentially increase his alone time.

"No, I'll be fine downstairs," he said. "I like having that space for myself."

I said okay—I feared making him angry with me. That evening and night, Jeff and I took turns checking on him. Each time we checked, he was sleeping hard.

The next morning, Jeff drove Sam to Summit Ridge Hospital so that he could be admitted at nine, per the instructions from the caseworker at Ridgeview. The hospital confirmed that he had to attend all day every day until they made the determination to release him.

While they were gone, I tackled necessary tasks: getting Sam's prescriptions filled, setting up an appointment with a psychiatrist whom Sam was to see on a regular basis, and calling Dr. R., the talk therapist Sam had seen before, to set up new weekly sessions. As I ticked off these to-do items, I felt more competent than I had any day since Labor Day.

A little after ten o'clock, Jeff arrived home with Sam in tow. Sam went to the basement without a word. Jeff told me that they had completed the admission process, but Sam was to start the next day instead of today. Sam, he said, had sunk back into a depressive state on their way home. We both went downstairs to talk to him.

He was lying on his stomach with his head turned. His right eye had tears in its corner. I sat beside him and stroked his hair. Jeff stood on the other side of the bed.

He rolled over onto his back and asked, "Mom, has anyone ever told you that I might have Asperger's?"

"No, what makes you ask that?"

"I could tell by the line of questioning at the hospital this morning, that was what their assumption was."

I felt annoyed that the intake evaluator had had this impression of Sam. I knew several people on the spectrum but had never thought that Sam exhibited any of the symptoms. Maybe this was a typical round of questioning for struggling smart boys and men, I reasoned. I tried to reassure Sam by saying he'd always met his milestones, had never lost any language skills, and had never exhibited any type of stimming. I told him that even if he was on the spectrum—which is vast and varied—he was so high-functioning that he would be fine. "Think of today's billionaires—Bill Gates, Mark Zuckerberg, Jeff Bezos. Certainly, they all exhibit mannerisms associated with Asperger's and all have been tremendously successful. "

Jeff joked that he himself stimmed—sometimes tapping his foot repeatedly or playing with his hair, especially when concentrating on something. "And I've done all right, haven't I?" We were trying whatever we could to rouse Sam from his depressive state—his wellbeing was so fragile. Sam gave Jeff a weak smile and said he wanted to sleep.

When Sam came upstairs later that afternoon, I told him about the appointments I had made and asked if I could monitor and dispense his medications, as the hospital had recommended. He said adamantly that he wanted to take charge of his illness and wouldn't abuse the drugs. He had made a commitment to be clean, and he would stick with it. Although I was nervous about the fact that I would not have any oversight into whether he was taking his medication, I agreed to his plan.

He seemed to be at loose ends that afternoon. As I worked, he occasionally wandered from the family room to the kitchen to my office, not saying much. I was looking for a way to cheer him and happened to have a $50 gift card to J.Crew sitting on my desk. I asked if he wanted to take it to the mall to get himself something. He said yes. Although I was nervous that he would be out on his own, I felt I needed to show some faith in his ability to manage alone.

When he returned a few hours later, I asked what he'd gotten. He showed me a belt. "Is that all you bought?" I asked. He said it was—that he'd needed a new belt. My heart filled my throat. I knew a belt was one of the things they took away at the hospital because of the risk of using it for self-harm. I struggled with how to react to his purchase. I ended up not saying anything. Sam took his new belt downstairs, and I went upstairs to my bedroom and cried out to God about my feelings of hopelessness. I asked God to see to Sam's survival, as, evidently, I could not.

Sam started the partial hospitalization at Summit Ridge the next day. Most days, when he returned, he seemed okay. He would reassure us that he would never take his life, that he had learned a great deal about himself and depression from the attempt and subsequent hospitalization. Still, I was ever vigilant. Each time I walked down the stairs to his room, I was terrified that I would find him dead.

SAM RESUMED SEEING Dr. R. on a weekly basis. He also started seeing the psychiatrist I'd found, Dr. V. I went with him for his first appointment with Dr. V. A friend who had struggled with her daughter's bipolar disorder had recommended that I attend all psychiatrist visits, since they pertained to the medications and it was always a good idea to have a second set of eyes and ears when dealing with psych meds. That first visit, Sam did not object to me going with him.

On the day of that first appointment with Dr. V., Sam and I first saw her PA. We sat in a private room and she asked Sam a series of questions, during which he revealed that he was not happy at Tech.

She said to Sam, "You are a nice-looking young man, personable, seemingly kind, and successful, with so many accomplishments. I think you need a virtual mirror to look into and honestly see yourself. You are doing well at a prestigious school, Georgia Tech. Where did you want to go to school, Harvard?"

"Yes."

Later, when the PA left and Dr. V. came in, she continued in the same vein. She looked over the PA's notes and tried to convince Sam that if he had been attending school away from Atlanta, the depression would probably still have occurred, but he would not have had his parents there to help him. I found it peculiar that both she and her PA were lasering in on Sam not getting into an Ivy. That fact was certainly not the only reason Sam suffered from depression.

She had me step outside the office for a few minutes while she spoke with Sam alone. After 15 minutes, I was invited to join them in the doctor's office. Dr. V. said that Sam was not severely depressed and that the hospital had him over-medicated. She told him to stop taking Abilify.

I was not impressed by Dr. V. She told us that she did not often see patients as high-functioning as Sam, and I was concerned about her dismissive attitude toward his illness. After just a few more appointments with her, she took Sam off Trileptal and Lexapro, kept him on Seroquel, and started him on Effexor. She never spoke with the psychiatrists at Ridgeview and never spoke with Sam's psychologist. If I knew then what I know now, I would have seen how perilous her quick switch of his medicines was.

This time, I did not ignore my uneasiness. I asked friends for recommendations and researched different psychiatrists. I found one with availability who came well-recommended and asked Sam if I could make an appointment for him to see her. He refused. He claimed he was doing fine with Dr. V.

JEFF AND I continued to be watchful over Sam: monitoring his moods, trying to cut down on his alone time, and covering him with our love. Jeff suggested that Sam do volunteer work with charitable organizations. As Jeff said, helping others is the best way to feel better about yourself. Sam took to this idea, and after completing his outpatient program, he became a Lunchtime Reading Mentor at a DeKalb County school, Dresden Elementary. He was paired with a sweet boy named Joshua, who would draw pictures for Sam. The two of them bonded, and Sam also began tutoring kids and teens at the local YMCA and volunteering at the local SPCA shelter. During these weeks when he was volunteering, he seemed to be more optimistic and less anxious. I felt hopeful and was grateful for Jeff's suggestion.

During this time, Sam was also swimming laps regularly at a nearby county pool, seeing his therapist weekly, and seeing his psychiatrist twice a month. I went with him for the first few psychiatrist visits, but then Sam asked me not to go and said he would handle it himself. It was the push/pull I had come to accept as part of our dynamic. I relented.

He continued to see his psychologist, Dr. R., but Jeff wanted to try something in addition to traditional therapies. For a few years, Jeff had been studying the benefits of hypnotherapy and reiki. I was mostly ignorant to what Jeff had learned but was willing to do anything to keep Sam alive. Jeff found the Wellspring Rejuvenation Center in Atlanta. The owner, Brad, performed reiki healing, hypnotherapy, and what he called "intuitive life coaching."

I took a look at Brad's website. He appeared to be a regular guy—brown hair and a beard and mustache speckled with gray, an infectious smile. *What harm could it do,* I thought.

I gave Jeff my blessing. When he approached Sam about taking this path to help treat his depression, Sam was accepting of the idea. This surprised me. For a long time, Sam had seen things as concrete, black and white. He didn't hold a high regard for a spiritual realm. I took his agreeing to do the reiki and hypnotherapy as a good sign that he wanted very much to get better.

The application Jeff filled out to make an appointment for Sam with Brad is a glimpse, in Jeff's voice, of Sam's state at the time, as well as how Jeff (and I) saw—and still see—Sam.

What has motivated you to seek help for Sam at this time?

Thoughts of suicide are the major motivators here. These may stem from perceived social rejection, perceived failures in life, and general anxiety. I say perceived because Sam is hard on himself. He has always been somewhat of an introvert, and this may make him think he will never be socially successful. Sam also tends to over-analyze himself, and that feeds the negative thoughts.

He does not deal with any type of failure very well. This started at a young age even with sports. He would prefer not to compete rather than face the possibility of losing.

When I asked him why he would consider suicide, he replied that he felt he did not fit into this world very well. That he did not have a reason to live.

For a couple of years, Sam has taken to self-medicating to feel good. This is only a very short-term solution with potentially disastrous side effects, especially for a student at GA Tech.

When you meet Sam, you will realize that he is a good-looking, intelligent person who should be enjoying life to the fullest.

Sam had two or three sessions with Brad, but he never revealed much to us about them. We mostly asked how the meetings made him feel. He said that he felt good and thought the process was positive.

Since Sam's death, I've listened to the recording from his January hypnotherapy session. One of the affirmations Brad suggested to Sam during hypnosis was, "You are worth loving because you are, not because of what you accomplish." Others included:

- True perfection is an illusion.
- It's okay to make mistakes while learning. You need to forgive yourself for any mistakes in the past.
- Be willing to ask for help when needed.

Listening to this recording reinforced the feelings I had about Sam's struggle within. He was just too hard on himself.

When Sam started seeing Brad, I was dubious about the merits of alternative therapies, including hypnotherapy. I tried not to convey this to Sam. Jeff and I were willing to do anything to help him learn to manage his depression.

There is no more helpless feeling in this world than trying to keep your child from harming or killing himself. No matter the number of times we told Sam that his suicide would destroy us, he could not comprehend that, not really. I believe he couldn't see beyond the actual moment he would kill himself. How at that moment he would be released from imagined unbearable pressure and expectation.

THROUGHOUT THE FALL of 2015, I kept track of treatment for Sam's depression. He continued to see his therapist weekly, but the frequency of psychiatrist visits was dropped to once per month. He saw Brad. We talked with Sam anytime he gave us a chance.

The remainder of the year was incredibly trying. Jeff and I committed to being as vigilant about Sam's moods and actions as we could possibly be, but he regularly brushed us off, leaving us feeling powerless.

I gradually began to confide in just a few close friends about Sam's suicide attempt and subsequent hospitalization. Initially, I wanted to keep this quiet both to protect Sam's privacy and because I worried that people would start to see him and us in a different way. Eventually, holding this distress internally became too much. Besides family, Angela was one of the first people I told. I was confident that my family and the friends I chose to tell would not be judgmental, and I was right. I felt some relief in letting a few people in.

I felt Sam was trying when, in early October, he said he was having symptoms of irritable bowel syndrome and gave me a list of foods he could and could not eat. Over the course of Sam's life, I'd become accustomed to trying to accommodate his diet. For several years, he had been either a vegetarian or a pescatarian. I looked at this most recent request from him as a positive sign: *If he wants to take good care of his body, he must want to live a healthy life.*

Later in October, I began to feel that Sam was slipping back into a depressive state. We searched for ways to keep him engaged. One weekend that month, Jeff asked him what he would enjoy doing. They settled on skeet shooting. They drove to a place in Etowah, Georgia, did target shooting, and had lunch. Jeff remembers Sam as being happy that day. Jeff also asked Sam to go on a fishing trip with him the first week in November, but Sam said he didn't want to go.

Over the next week, Sam was having trouble getting out of bed. I could not plead enough nor bribe him enough to get him up. One day that week, out of desperation, I called Jeff at work. Jeff came home and got Sam out of bed, and they went for a walk. When they returned, Sam complained about his hip hurting. I told him that was probably from spending too much time in bed, lying on his side. Even so, I arranged an appointment for him with a massage therapist I occasionally use.

Sam went to the massage appointment. He came home afterward and said he felt somewhat better—mentally and physically. I asked him if the therapist had spoken of spiritual things with him, as she had with me before. Sam said she had, but it was okay.

I broached the subject of additional volunteer opportunities. I researched and found that a local food bank needed help that same day. With just a little prodding, he went and spent much of the day there. Arriving home that first day, he seemed energized by the experience. Sam seemed happier and more alive than he had in months. He smilingly told me that the difference between working there and at a place like the SPCA was that the food bank had no one completing court-mandated community service. Everyone was there because they wanted to be there.

In the middle of October, we were to go to my nephew's wedding in east Tennessee. Sam asked to stay home, but I insisted he needed to be with us. We booked two rooms in a hotel. Sam and the girls shared a room and seemed to get along well. The day of the wedding, Sam was in a good mood and talked easily and comfortably with his grandparents, aunts, uncles, and cousins. My sweet 22-year-old niece asked Sam to dance with her, but he declined. I wish he had given himself the freedom to just be, and not to always be contained and controlled. But, then again, that would not have been the sober Sam.

The next day, the five of us drove to Asheville. We spent the morning walking leisurely through an arts festival downtown. Sam was affable and talkative with the artisans and purchased a small handmade pottery bowl. The bowl was about three inches in diameter and glazed in various shades of brown. I wasn't sure of its intended use, but weeks later, I found remnants of pot in it.

After visiting the festival, we had a great lunch at Farm Burger. Finishing our high-calorie meal, we were all getting tired, and the girls were complaining to go home. We walked back to our car. As we were leaving the Asheville parking garage, Jeff and I got into an argument about how to get out of the garage and what the best route home was. I was anxious, and, as usual, my anxiety manifested itself in anger.

Sam, in the back seat of the van, was talking to his sisters. They were playing a card game. Sam seemed unusually animated. On an impulse, I turned to the back of the minivan and asked, "Sam, are you high?"

He said he wasn't, and he was furious with me for accusing him. What was wrong with me? I had promised just a month before that I would get help with just this sort of thing, but at the first minorly stressful incident, I had developed into a shrew. I was projecting my anxiety as rage. I apologized, but the three-hour car ride passed in relative silence.

The following Thursday, October 22, 2015, was Sam's twentieth birthday. I had made reservations a month earlier at Gunshow, a well-reviewed restaurant in Atlanta. During the day, the girls were at school and Jeff was at work. Sam asked if he could go to Tech to hang out with some friends and then meet us at the restaurant. I agreed.

Sam arrived at the restaurant just a little late. He seemed solemn but not despondent. When I asked whom he had seen at Tech, he responded with a vague "friends." He was a little engaged during the meal, but not as much as I would have hoped. He would answer our questions and smile halfheartedly, but he didn't seem happy. I wondered if he felt let down because he was spending his twentieth birthday dinner with family instead of friends.

After dinner, we went back home for gift-giving. I had made a modest attempt at a scrapbook for Sam that included news clippings and pictures of him over the last 20 years. Typical of me, I had only started it the day before — it was really kind of a mess. He thanked me for the scrapbook and, acknowledging its unpolished state, told me he appreciated my effort. I had also made him a birthday cake. Sam's favorite candy had always been Butterfinger. I had found a recipe for a Butterfinger cake and made that for him. I don't recall if it was any good. He seemed annoyed and bothered as we sang "Happy Birthday" to him. We couldn't get him to smile for the pictures and video. He looked like he just wanted it over. After presents and cake, he descended the stairs back into the basement. I felt guilty that I hadn't created a better celebration for him.

CHAPTER 19

Sam's Writing

Taken from Journals / Cell Phone

*M*onday, 9/21/15:
  Ten things to remember:

1. *Thoughts are ephemeral.*
2. *We can and do choose the thoughts we act on.*
3. *Thoughts are communicated in language.*
4. *Words, once they are expressed, lead to feelings. (The thought almost always comes before the feeling. When feeling negative, notice what you are thinking about.)*
5. *Our feelings affect motivation.*
6. *Our motivation affects action, and action is EVERYTHING.*
7. *Actions we take or don't take, lead to results.*
8. *Energy shows itself to where you pay attention.*
9. *What we focus on flourishes.*
10. *Forgiveness is the process of repetitive intention (instead of focusing on hurt/judgment, focus on lessons learned).*

Wednesday, 9/22/15:

1. *I have many good qualities.*
2. *Others perceive me as a good and likeable person.*
3. *I deserve the respect of others.*
4. *I love myself just the way I am.*
5. *I don't have to be perfect to be loved.*

Friday, 10/2/15:
Depression sucks. Nothing is really holding my interest right now. All my friends are in school, so there isn't shit for me to do except work, volunteer, play video games, listen to music, or screw around on the computer. It's difficult to find the drive to do only independent studying that would be useful if I am to return to school next semester. I still have plenty of time to get back on my feet, though. I still have a few weeks until the new SSRI kicks in, so things should start looking up for me. I really want to get high right now. I may try to find some local herb… or not… I really need to detox. But, then again, my days of dependency on tree are behind me. I could trust myself to only use occasionally. I'll just have to do so under the radar because my parents would flip out.

It's only natural to want to "get away" every once-in-a-while. When I'm out and about, I usually feel pretty okay though my introverted tendencies will tire me out eventually. But, when I'm stuck at home, I feel pretty insufferable. Smoking would temporarily relieve these feelings. I really just need something to hold me for the next few weeks, and with weed, the risk for continued dependency is low. Ideally, I'd like to be in a position where I don't need weed at all, and I'm hoping that the antidepressant will do that, but in the meantime, I really just want to be able to enjoy the things I used to, like movies and music. I can't do that in my current state of mind.

I found it funny and sad how the psychiatrist claimed that almost all weed is laced; like, what the fuck? How do you even back such a claim? Economically it makes no sense to lace a drug. If anything, drugs are more likely to be diluted as you move down the supply chain, e.g., Young Scooter turning half a brick to a whole brick. Furthermore, it's not like I'm buying this shit on the corner; I get it shipped straight from the grower, who has a reputation to upkeep. Makes you wonder. Same deal with the handout I received at Ridgeview that cites a disproven claim that cannabis reduces IQ by 8 points. Hell, they even diagnosed me with drug-induced psychosis because I smoked weed that morning. I was definitely in a state of psychosis, but that was because of stress and lack of sleep. Frankly, I tire of this Nixon-era ignorance. Especially when it comes from the people who dictate my meds.

I wonder how long I've actually been depressed. I've had suicidal thoughts as far back as middle school and piss-poor self-esteem for as long as I can remember. I've just kept everything bottled up until now. Eh, better late than never I suppose.

Sunday, 10/4:
So, I definitely have IBS. It's embarrassing to admit, but it's true. Therefore, I need to really watch my diet. Furthermore, exercise is now doubly important for me. It both manages IBS symptoms, as well as regulates stress, that in turn reduces IBS symptoms. Also, I really need to get off caffeine. I'm pretty dependent, that makes it difficult, but dependence is another reason I need to quit. Also, anything that increases appetite and lowers inhibitions (you know what I'm talking about) is probably best to be avoided. To manage these symptoms, I've made a food spreadsheet in Excel and a list of foods that I should and shouldn't eat.

I've already quit a bunch of things these past few weeks. Might as well stop some bad foods while I'm at it.

Monday, 10/5:
It's midnight. I don't really know what I want to write about. Music is sounding good right now. I oughta move my speakers back downstairs. Sometimes I like having the subwoofer; it fits some kinds of music. I started the Boogie Play All Access trial today, so I'll see how that goes.

Being back in Suwanee is boring. I wish the Kratom would come in already, but USPS is a bunch of pussies. Doesn't their motto have something to do with delivering in spite of the weather? It's not even raining that badly. If it doesn't get here today, Ima be pissed. Well, I'm going to bed now.

Tuesday, 10/6:
I'm bored. But I don't want to do anything right now, so I'll stay bored. Even though I was at risk of becoming addicted to Kratom, I regret having

given it up temporarily. It would at least give me something to alleviate boredom. It's good at that. I get overwhelmed very easily. Hopefully, the antidepressant will help with that. Hmmm…I don't feel like writing anything else.

Thursday, 10/8:
Anhedonia sucks. My symptoms have gotten worse this week. I think it's because I've been smoking more cigarettes. I've smoked six per day since Friday. It could be because I haven't done Kratom since Friday. I feel indifferent, irritable, or sad toward everything, so I'm basically anhedonic. Which sucks. The good news is that I have a kitten sleeping in my lap.

Thursday, 10/15:
Today was a good day. I volunteered at the food bank from 10 a.m.—2 p.m., that was very enjoyable and rewarding. I was also buzzed off of Kratom the entire time. Although being drugged up wasn't the best idea, I needed something to dull my hip pain, which the Kratom actually did very well. I think I'm getting addicted to Kratom, though. I've gone through almost 20g in less than 3 days. Honestly, I don't really mind; Kratom is dirt cheap and has very mild withdrawal symptoms. Plus, unlike weed, I'm actually functional on Kratom. In fact, I was able to learn physics while on 7g. Addiction could definitely be problematic down the road, but for now, I don't want to worry any more than I have to.

Friday, 10/16:
So today, I met a homeless man. While I was outside a gas station smoking a cig, he asked if he could bum one. He seemed sweet and was very apologetic, so I started talking to him. His name is a combination of his parents' names that I can't remember, but he went by "Ga." He is 26 and has nothing to his name. His father has been in jail since he was 6. I gave him the little cash I had on hand and bought him a meal from Dunkin

Donuts. It wasn't much, but he was incredibly grateful. He's not a bum; he's a kind, warm-hearted person victimized by circumstance, and most of his society, his fellow human beings, won't ever give him a second look. He told me he was suicidal.

It's a fucked-up world we live in when a young man's only options are to beg or die. He's not able to enter a group home because he's from North Carolina and has no identification. Seriously, America?! I wish the best for him.

I should write a North Avenue Review article about this subject in hopes of it opening a few eyes. I can't deny that I have a good heart and a high sense of empathy. That is without a doubt.

Dr. R. suggested creating backup plans. If this whole college thing doesn't work out, I'll devote my life to helping people like Ga. Actually, after I graduate, I want to go to a third world country and help people out there for a year. Because there is no better high than doing for others, and I've done Molly.

Sunday, 10/18:
We went to East Tennessee to celebrate my cousin Mark's wedding. The weather was nice, and we stopped in Asheville on the way home. We had a great lunch and walked around an art fair. Then mom decided to lose her shit with Dad, about driving, directions, whatever. I guess I was talking with my sisters a little animatedly because they seemed an open audience. At one point, Mom turned around and asked if I was high. I had used Kratom but was so pissed that she asked that. Why does she leap to assume the worst, even when it's true? In my pissed off state, I made a note in my phone.

What to tell my sisters

You have many good qualities
You have low self esteem because of mom's criticism and behavioral example
You tend to isolate because of this
You have perfectionist qualities
You can get easily irritated
I was/am the same
I was excessively critical, angry, and self-loathing
I had difficulty in social relationships and felt self-conscious around women especially
Give examples
I was mean toward yall when I was younger
I was spiteful toward Dad because of Mom's influence.
I developed self-destructive coping habits
Tell about suicide attempt and what landed me in hospital.
Listen more to dad, he's less fucked in the head
Be confident and happy with who you are
You can always talk to me. I've been through this shit.

Last modified: Oct 18, 2015

Sunday, 10/28/15:

I didn't think I would ever be suicidal again, but here I am. I really want to die. Ideally, I'd want to die of a heroin overdose, but to do that, I'd have to wait until I'm back in school. I don't want to get better; I just want a way out. I just want to sleep forever. My entire life has been tortuous, and no amounts of meds or counseling will fix that. I hate myself and the world I inhabit. To be truthful, when, or how I die means nothing once I'm dead, so I might as well get it over with. Although I'd prefer to step out quietly, going out with a bang wouldn't be that bad either. Accessibility supersedes romanticization.

CHAPTER 20

Thanksgiving and Christmas 2015

In August, just weeks before we'd learned of Sam's mental illness, we'd planned a family vacation to the Florida Keys for the week of Thanksgiving. Normally we would have spent the holiday with Jeff's mother and brother in Tuscaloosa, Alabama, where his mother lives. Thanks to the Netflix original *Bloodline,* I had become interested in visiting the Keys. I'd booked us a rental on the canal on Key Colony Beach. The house was owned by a couple who lived on the island and owned two homes there. The house was one-story with three bedrooms, two baths, and a large deck looking over the canal. Originally, the plan had been for Jeff, Maggie, Claire, and me to drive down on Saturday and for Sam to then fly from Atlanta to Miami on the Wednesday before Thanksgiving, after his last classes before break.

By mid-September, Jeff wanted to cancel the trip. We had just paid $4,000 out-of-pocket to Ridgeview for Sam's week-long stay there. I knew that Jeff was right that we didn't have the extra funds to afford the trip, but I was adamant that we all needed this time together and something to look forward to. Jeff acquiesced.

Since Sam had taken medical withdrawal from Tech for the semester, there was no longer a reason for him to fly, and he rode with us. The drive there was bearable, and we made it in twelve hours. Sam slept most of the way, didn't engage with us, and had to be wakened for lunch and rest stops.

Once we arrived at Key Colony Beach, we relaxed into beach-living mode. The rental turned out to be within walking distance of a park perfect for watching sunsets. The house came with bicycles, so at the end of each day of our vacation, we would all walk or ride bikes down to see the sunset.

Sam, Maggie, and Claire at Key Colony Beach

There were several mornings on our vacation when we had trouble getting Sam out of bed. But once up, he seemed okay. He listened to his music out on the deck overlooking the canal and went with us to a sea turtle hospital and on a day trip to Key West. One day, he went with me to the club pool that overlooked the ocean. We had our Thanksgiving meal at a restaurant on the beach. Sam seemed genuinely happy when a manatee came up to our deck off the canal and spent an extended visit with us.

During the evenings, we would play games or watch movies. Sometimes Sam would get on his computer and vape. Naturally, Sam hated my music, and I did not care for his. We had debates over this, but it was all amicable. One evening, Sam asked what we wanted for Christmas, and all of us said we didn't need much, just any little thing. I did say I'd like a speaker like he had to play music from my phone, but only if it wasn't too expensive.

The week passed too fast. Our uneventful, twelve-hour drive down seemed to have jinxed us, and the return trip was excruciating.

We should have expected as much—it was the Saturday after Thanksgiving and the day of the football game between the University of Florida and Florida State in Gainesville. I suggested stopping somewhere and staying overnight and then completing the drive in the morning. Jeff and the kids wanted to push through and just get home.

We asked Sam to drive at one point, to give Jeff and me a break. He agreed but drove too quickly and recklessly, and it was dark. After twenty minutes or so, Jeff told him to pull over and let him drive. For the remainder of the 16-hour drive, Sam sat in the back of the van and seemed to sleep. Around eleven o'clock Saturday evening, we pulled into our garage. *Home sweet home,* I thought. As Sam exited the van, he said aloud, "I just want to kill myself."

I took his arm. "Sam, why? We are all tired and tomorrow will be better," I said. "Please, tell me how I can help you?"

"You can't," he said, and he went inside and down to the basement.

IN EARLY DECEMBER, Sam returned to his job delivering pizzas. We didn't object. I would occasionally "take the temperature" of Sam's mood. I felt his meds weren't right, but his psychiatrist stuck to what she had prescribed. Sam wouldn't let me go to these appointments; for all I knew, he could have been telling Dr. V. that he felt good.

I began Christmas shopping that year with little enthusiasm. I bought Sam a parka he wanted and opened a Roth IRA for him. I bought the girls and Jeff things off their lists as well. On Friday, December 18, I was in my office tying up loose ends with work before the holidays when Sam came in and said he needed to wrap Christmas gifts. I told him the gift-wrapping supplies were in my bedroom. He went upstairs. Something about his manner unsettled me, so after 20 minutes, I went upstairs to check on him. He had wrapping paper out but had not started wrapping any gifts. He was staring into the middle distance (doing this, I later read, is a sign not just of depression but of suicidal ideation). I sat down on the floor with him and asked if he needed my help wrapping. He sat there quietly while I wrapped the gifts for him. I asked him to tell me what was wrong. I knew he was in a sad state, but he would only say he was okay. He later went downstairs.

Feeling rattled, I called Jeff at work, telling him Sam seemed very despondent, and I asked whether he could come home early and do something with him. I suggested the new Star Wars movie, and Jeff said he'd buy tickets online. A couple of hours afterward, we learned that Sam was scheduled to work delivering pizzas later that afternoon and into the evening. Jeff took a neighbor with him to the movie instead.

After Sam left for work, I went into the basement and began going through every drawer and space in his desk, bureau, and closet, looking for perhaps drugs or some clue about his dysphoria. My heart was pounding. Call it mother's intuition, but I knew Sam was in a perilous place. I did not have the password to get into his computer. I scoured his room. I found a yellow legal pad he'd been using as a journal. Four or five pages in, I found a folded note. There was no date on it.

So sorry to be leaving in such an abrupt manner, but it really is time that I get going. I've greatly overstayed my welcome on this world. Whether or not you agree with me, I find a serene beauty in throwing it all away.

I ran for my phone and called Sam. He answered, and I told him I'd found the note and was terribly frightened. He said he was fine and at work. I told him to please come home right now. He was dismissive and said he'd be okay. I kept insisting and wanting to go get him, but he just put me off, saying he had to go make a delivery.

I got in touch with Jeff after the movie ended and told him what I had found and that Sam had refused to come home from work. He went to the pizza restaurant and insisted Sam come home. Sam told him, "I don't have anything to do it with, anyway," meaning a way to commit suicide. He did not deny the note, nor its implication.

In the time between when I found the note and when Jeff found Sam, Maggie came to me and asked what was going on. She had heard part of my phone conversation with Jeff and knew something was wrong. She could tell from my tears and jitteriness how scared I was. I decided it was time to be honest with her. I told her about the note, and I told her about Sam's attempt in September. She began to cry. Months after Sam's death, I found Maggie's journal entry from this day. When I first read it, I felt crushed. But I was also reminded of how Maggie's life was transformed during Sam's illness and death. It was not just me who agonized and suffered.

December 18, 2015

Dear Diary,
Mom found a suicide note from Sam when he went out to go to work at Cooley's Pizza. I am so scared, and Dad just left to go look for him. I've been crying, and I thought if I'd write everything down that I maybe would feel better.

Then I realized how truly selfish I am. I'm writing to make myself feel better when Sam is God knows where planning God knows what.

Dear God, bring Sam home safely. Dad must have left 20 or 30 minutes ago. It is now 7:00. I don't even know what to do with myself. If I let myself be okay for a second, I know I'll hate myself in the future.

How could I possibly watch tv when my brother is out there somewhere planning to kill himself?! I am SO SCARED. I love Sam so much.

When Jeff and Sam returned home, the three of us talked at length. I felt strongly that we needed to readmit Sam into the hospital the next day. He said he'd be okay and was vehemently opposed to going back to the hospital. I told him that we would talk about it in the morning.

I hardly slept that night and more than once went downstairs to check on him. In the morning, after a lengthy debate, he grudgingly agreed to go to the hospital. Jeff took him to Summit Ridge for an evaluation. Jeff told me when they got home that the evaluator had really wanted to admit Sam, but Sam would not allow it. Eventually they agreed on another outpatient hospitalization.

I was as terrified as I had been the first time he'd been in Ridgeview in September, and I begged him to move his stuff upstairs to his old bedroom. He kept reassuring me that he was okay. That Monday, four days before Christmas, he started partial hospitalization at Summit Ridge.

CHAPTER 21

Hannah

The first time I met Hannah was on December 23, at a family session at Summit Ridge Hospital—a different hospital from the one where Sam had completed his inpatient hospitalization (Ridgeview), but the same one where he had completed his September outpatient treatment. Sam was undergoing the first week of his two-week outpatient hospitalization—Monday through Friday, 8:30 a.m. to 3:30 p.m. Once per week, family members were invited to come to the hospital and ask questions during special sessions.

As it had been when Jeff and I had attended the parent session in late September, the meeting room was set up with a long conference table and chairs on all sides. Hannah sat next to Sam. Her sister and mother were on her left. At the time, I didn't have reason to think much about her. (In fact, I would not even learn her name until later.) I was unaware of if they had chosen to sit together or if that was just happenstance. I sat on Sam's right side, in between him and Claire. Jeff and I had attended a family session at this same hospital when Sam had been there in September, but Jeff was absent this time because he was gathering his mother from Tuscaloosa so she could spend Christmas with us. Claire had agreed to go with me to support her brother.

The meeting was conducted by the same group leader as the September meeting. He talked most of the time in a painfully monotone voice, mostly about bipolar disorder. His spiel was almost identical to the one he had given in September. I tuned him out and, out of the corner of my eye, watched Sam and Hannah interact.

Hannah seemed unsettled, but Sam was calm. She took a pencil and dug it into the veneer on the side of the long table in front of us. Pieces of the veneer flaked off and fell to the floor. As Hannah obsessively attacked the table, her sister tried to stop her by gently placing her hand over Hannah's hand. Hannah flicked away her sister's hand and continued to furiously dig.

Sam would lean toward Hannah occasionally and whisper things to her. I couldn't hear what was said, but I sensed a connection between them. I thought that Sam was much better functioning than this girl with her tattoo, pierced nose, and large pink glasses that hid her face but magnified her eyes. Her entire demeanor gave off an air of bitterness and resentment. When her mother tried to speak to her, Hannah determinedly looked in the opposite direction. At the end of the meeting, Sam made no attempt to introduce us to Hannah. He talked with her a short while and then came over to us.

Claire and I hugged Sam and told him we were headed back home. He said he would be there later.

SAM WAS DOING PHP during the holidays, but that didn't change much about our annual routine. We had started spending the holiday at home after a Christmas when Sam was seven and his big gift was a foosball table that didn't arrive at my parents' house intact. A broken gift from Santa just didn't cut it. After that, we had created our own traditions, including attending our neighbors' annual Christmas Eve party, a large Christmas breakfast, and hosting a nice evening meal on Christmas Day for Jeff's family. The day after Christmas, we would generally travel to west Tennessee to see my family.

Jeff's mom spent the holiday with us. Sam was overly generous with the gifts he gave each of us. He must have gone through most of the money in his checking account. I'm sure the Bluetooth speaker and the Alexander Wang t-shirt he gave me totaled over $200. I had fulfilled just a portion of the wish list Sam had given me, all of which was high-end designer clothes and shoes. Sam didn't have a lot of apparel, but what he had was of good quality.

Midday on Christmas, I could sense his restlessness, and I asked if he wanted to go with me to see the new Star Wars movie. I was happy when he said yes. We drove to a nearby deserted mall and bought tickets. We sat near the front of the theater and were both engrossed in the film. It seemed much like old times; over the last several months, it had been rare that we had felt entirely comfortable in each other's presence. On the car ride home, we talked easily about the movie.

At home, Jeff and I fixed a holiday meal of beef tenderloin, scallops, asparagus, and stuffed potatoes. I made a chocolate yule log cake. I had never made this dessert before and was pleased when it came out as intended. (Baking has never been my strong suit.) Besides Jeff's mom, Jeff's brother David and his wife Donna joined us for dinner. We let Sam have a glass of wine, and he seemed content—actively engaging in conversation. Seeing Sam enjoying Christmas made me hopeful that the current part-time hospitalization was working.

Two days after Christmas, I took Maggie and Claire to Tennessee to see my family. We wanted Sam to continue to attend PHP. His doctors did not think he should be released for at least another week, and Jeff stayed in Suwanee to enforce this.

Maggie, Claire, and I spent a few days in my hometown. I don't remember much about this visit. I'm sure we exchanged gifts with family and had a potluck meal with my parents, my siblings, and their families. We only stayed two days. On the way home, while I was driving on I-75, Jeff called. I spoke to him over my car's Bluetooth.

"I'll have dinner ready for you guys when you get here," Jeff said. "And Sam has a friend over."

"What friend?"

"Some girl."

"Some girl he met at the hospital? Is it a date?" Jeff said he didn't think so; Sam had described her explicitly as a friend.

We arrived home and met the girl. It was Hannah.

She and Sam played video games downstairs in the basement, then joined the rest of us for dinner. Hannah didn't engage much in our dinner-table conversation, answering our open-ended questions about school and family briefly. I'm guilty of making snap judgments based on first impressions, but there was a vibe about Hannah that troubled me. However, she and Sam seemed to be enjoying each other's company—frequently smiling at one another. Later, I asked Jeff if he felt uneasy about Hannah's demeanor, and he said he didn't. Maggie and Claire said they liked her. Maybe it was just me.

Hannah was still at our house, hanging out in the basement with Sam, when Jeff and I went to bed.

"How was your date?" I asked Sam the next morning as he ascended the stairs from the basement. I was sitting in the family room, drinking coffee and reading the news on my phone. Jeff was in the adjoining kitchen. I had meant my question in jest, since Sam had stressed that they were only friends.

"It was okay."

Jeff interjected that Sam had told him it hadn't been a date, but Sam said it had become that way.

The time with Hannah in our lives was rocky. There seemed to be some near crisis with her almost every day. She told us she suffered from bipolar disorder. She also seemed prone to dependency. Hannah had to be with Sam all the time, and when he was at school or at work or wanted to be with friends without her, she would call and text him relentlessly. I believe she was looking to Sam to make her feel better. But, of course, Sam had his own internal demons.

At the beginning of the relationship, they seemed to spend every spare moment with one another. Hannah had been attending college outside Atlanta but was back living with her parents after her own attempted suicide. I communicated a few times via text with her mother. She seemed as concerned about Hannah as I was about Sam.

Hannah described her parents as hatefully controlling. She blamed them for setbacks she'd suffered. It became clear to me, as had been evident when she had been butchering that table with a pencil, that Hannah lived her life with a chip on her shoulder. I tried to keep my concerns from Sam. He seemed excited about the new relationship.

I did not know this at the time, but during Sam's second two-week outpatient program at Summit Ridge, he was still using drugs. In texts he sent Hannah, he talked about being released early one day from PHP because he was high. Jeff and I were never told by the hospital staff about this.

CHAPTER 22

Sam's Final Months

Sam started back at Georgia Tech in January for the spring semester, taking three classes and living at home. His course load included two upper-level physics classes and an introduction into psychology. I think perhaps he had chosen the psychology class to better understand his illness.

I prayed that getting back into college life would make Sam happier. Back in November, when registration had been due, Sam had procrastinated getting the necessary paperwork from the dean and the psychiatrist that would allow him to resume school. I encouraged him to re-enroll but to take only a workload that he could handle without too much stress.

I wanted him to have a more predictable schedule and to be held accountable. I thought attending school while living at home would be the best choice. Later, Sam's therapist told me that he had not believed Sam was ready to take classes. He had conveyed this to Sam, and they had been working on a plan for the short term that did not involve school. Dr. R. said it should have been him—not Dr. V., the psychiatrist—who signed the Tech paperwork. I wish I'd known. Still, Sam had known Dr. R.'s opinion and made the decision to enroll.

As the semester began, Sam stayed occupied with school, his pizza-delivery job, and Hannah. He drove to Tech and attended class daily—all without any prodding by me. It seemed to me that he was acting more contented and was less moody. For the first time in months, I felt hopeful. Still, I was always looking for signs of relapse. And, in fact, there was a scary drug relapse in early January.

Late one evening while I was drowsily watching television in the bedroom, Jeff came upstairs to tell me we needed to go get Sam. He had called to say he'd run out of gas. Jeff's normally calm demeanor was replaced with a palpable urgency. He was impatient as he told me to get my shoes on.

"How did he run out of gas?" I asked. I didn't believe that Jeff would be this intense if Sam had simply run out of gas.

We went out to the van, and Jeff continued, "He's with Hannah. He sounds wasted and scared." My stomach dropped.

Sam had told Jeff that they were in a church parking lot not far from Tallulah Gorge State Park, over an hour away. I'd had no idea that he had gone there that day. From the sign in front, Sam had given Jeff the name of the church, and, using Google Maps, we tracked them down. Jeff had brought a gas can from home, and we stopped at a gas station to fill it. When we reached Sam's car, we found Hannah lying in the back seat. Sam sat in the front passenger seat, head down and crying.

"Sam, what have you done?" I asked.

With tears in his voice, Sam replied, "We dropped acid and both of us had a bad trip. I got lost trying to get home and then we ran out of gas. I'm so sorry."

Jeff and I got Hannah out of the back seat and helped her to the van. She was babbling and emotional, too. Jeff drove Sam and Hannah to our house, while I followed in Sam's car.

When we walked in the door from the garage to the kitchen, Maggie ran to Sam and hugged him around his waist. I didn't know if Jeff had told her when we had left where we were going or if she had overheard us talking before leaving. We had left in such a hurry.

Slowly, Sam and Hannah began to come down. To make sure that the kids—especially Hannah—were all right, Jeff stayed awake and in the basement with the two of them. He later told me that Sam swore he would never again touch LSD. He realized how badly the night could have gone and that he could have ended up in jail or in a car crash, or that he and Hannah could have died.

The subsequent days were clouded by the scariness of Sam's actions. I thanked God for getting us through this without any permanent damage, but I had an overwhelming feeling of waiting for the next shoe to drop.

IN THE MIDDLE of January, I had an emergency appendectomy that required a two-night stay at Emory Hospital. I've wondered if my heightened stress during those months had something to do with the appendicitis. Jeff and the girls came to see me several times. Sam texted but never visited.

After being released, I went home to recuperate. Friends and family provided cards, flowers, and meals. Sam said to me, "Doesn't seem like getting your appendix out is all bad. You get flowers, food, and a prescription for Oxy." I immediately flushed the hydrocodone down the toilet.

One day later that month, I thought Sam might be high. I was watching for any word or action that might mean he'd broken his promise to us about LSD. On this day, his behavior seemed just a little off; he seemed evasive and vague when I tried to talk with him. While he was out of the house, I went into his bedroom and started snooping around. I looked in the obvious places and had just picked up a notebook with his writing in it when he and Hannah walked into the bedroom.

I looked at him and said, "I'm sorry," and I made a quick exit. Surprisingly, he didn't seem that upset to find me snooping, but, still, I worried that later he would unload on me for invading his privacy. I sent him a text explaining that I was sorry for snooping but had wanted to make sure he was doing okay. I said I had done it because of my tremendous love for him. He texted back, "Okay." I took his nonchalance as a good sign. He must not have had anything to hide. I was relieved that he treated this breach of trust gently.

The following Sunday, I checked our banking records. Sam's checking account was tied to mine, and so I could see his balance on the account's home page. I opened the details of Sam's account. The only thing that seemed odd was a $70 charge from a tattoo parlor. I texted him.

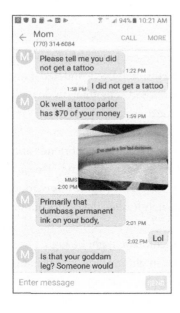

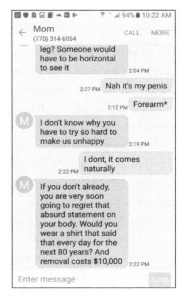

Sam's tattoo

It's obvious from the text exchange that I was upset. In retrospect, what's so awful about a tattoo? Nothing. Knowing Sam's taste for irony, I understood he mostly meant for it to be funny. Later, he confirmed that it was supposed to be humorous but also to remind to him to make better life choices. What could I say to that? Of course, I wanted him to strive to do better.

THE TATTOO DRAMA soon subsided, and our home life began a tentative return to its rhythm from before Sam's attempted suicide five months earlier—a pattern of minor ups and downs. We had meals at our house with Hannah, and I was beginning to grow—if not fond of—at least sympathetic toward her. Just as Sam had been diagnosed with depression and a substance-induced mood disorder, Hannah struggled to deal with being bipolar. In her own way, I felt that she showed a lot of love toward Sam, and for this I was grateful.

For the rest of January and the first weeks of February, Sam was attending classes and doing well in school. He was engaged with us, sober, and seemingly hopeful about his future. I began to feel like we could start to move forward, that he would be okay. I acknowledged to myself that Sam would probably always need to be on medication and get psychotherapy, but, for the first time in five months, I allowed myself to feel cautiously optimistic.

Although Sam and Hannah were inseparable during January and the first half of February, by late February, the bloom was off the rose. Sam began to try to create a little distance; he was beginning to feel trapped by her neediness. He asked our advice about breaking up with Hannah. My opinion was that it would be best to do it in person, to be kind, but to make it a clean break. I advised him to not leave any gray area about potentially remaining friends. I said this not to be mean to Hannah, but because I thought that was the kindest action in the long run.

Hannah had become unpredictable and needy. She made demands of Sam's time and his attention, and her insistence on wanting to always be with him was interfering with his schoolwork. Because he was always empathetic toward others, I could tell Sam was struggling with the idea of hurting her. He feared that she might hurt herself if he didn't handle the situation in the best way. In fact, she had told him as much—that if he left her, she would kill herself. In the end, this guilt was too much for Sam. On February 25, 2016, he drove to the woods near our house and took his life.

PART III

SEARCHING FOR HOPE

"I'm not afraid of death because I don't believe in it. It's just getting out of one car, and into another."

—JOHN LENNON

CHAPTER 23

My Journal

*F*riday, March 3, 2016

One week since.... I am so out of touch as to where I am and how I'm supposed to act. You would be amazed at how generous, in every way, friends, neighbors, and family have been.

My epiphany: People and community are ultimately good. The gifts of service, the abundance of food, the offers of prayer have meant so much.

Monday, March 6, 2016

Today I drove to Main Street and walked along the railroad tracks where we believe you walked on the day you died. I was trying to get a feel for your actions and thoughts, but I couldn't. I will not have any answers until we are together in the next life. Even so, I suspect your actions were impulsive, and therefore, avoidable. I wish I could have said or done ANYTHING to have changed the outcome. There will never be a day I don't doubt myself and wish I had done/been what you needed.

Wednesday, March 8, 2016

Today I spoke with Jackson's mom. She told me that Jackson and Michael, upon hearing of your death, sat on the phone with one another for three hours; not saying much, only crying in disbelief. I told your dad this story, and he began crying, too, and asked me, "Did Sam even know how much he was loved and admired?" I had no answer. Did you?

Did you have any idea how your death would impact so many other lives?

Eight of your high school classmates went out after the visitation to reminisce about you. My beautiful boy. I cannot pretend life will be recovered to any semblance of normalcy without you.

March 9, 2016

People do love to quote the Bible during the tragedies of life. Sad to say, most of what is relayed is not only not inspiring, but also not appropriate to our situation. People have sent me Bible verses urging me to praise God. Others have said it was the will of God that you died. What a horrible thing to speak to a grieving mother. And, right now, I don't feel too eager to praise God. He blew that when He let you die.

There were times when discussing (especially math and science-related) stuff, I could tell that my lack of knowledge was irritating to you. My brain worked fractionally as well as yours. But for me, this brought me a sense of pride. I took pride in your intellect, superior to mine; your physical beauty; your athletic prowess; your ability to see through those who were superficial. I feel the same way about Maggie and Claire. The thing a parent wants most in life is to produce offspring who are better.

March 10, 2016

Many visitors, many cards. Sweet cards from so many you may or may not remember. I wish you had had the opportunity to read these expressions of love for you, before your decision—it would have stopped you. This I know.

March 11, 2016

I think it's so beautiful that you are visiting Claire in her dreams. They are vivid and real and so comforting to her. She said that your appearance was ephemeral and spirit-like. You were happy, and that was so assuring to her.

And, of course, you have come to me in dreams, as well. I feel these are visitations with you and not just dreams. I can hear your voice talking to me, and I know it is you reaching from beyond this life.

Wednesday, March something
It's all a nightmare, so the days of the week and dates matter little.

Dad and I met with your psychologist, Dr. R. He confided you are the first patient he has ever lost. Dr. R. is so visibly affected by your death and perplexed about your timing. He said when he last saw you, the day before your suicide you seemed in good spirits and with a decisive plan to break up with Hannah, the following Sunday.

So, we are all wondering what happened. In that short amount of time, what happened? I can tell that Dr. R., like Dad and I, is struggling with a measure of guilt. Why couldn't we save you?

Saturday, March 12, 2016
Hi, Love, I'm meeting with Andy tomorrow at 8:00 a.m. at Starbucks. Seemingly he was the last person you spoke with. I just want to listen to what Andy says, even though I know there are no answers.

I just want to know what the turning point was. Was there a point I could have diverted you? Saving you for now? What I wouldn't give to have one more minute, one more day, one more year with you. I would give up all possessions, all luxuries, all necessities even — I crave the sight of your beautiful eyes, your half-smile, and your confident stance.

My God, Sam, I miss you so much. I wish I had been a better role model for you by getting better help for my own depression, but I feel safe in saying that you were born into a family that loved you, adored you, and would have dropped all to preserve your life. If I'd known for certain that I could kill myself and be with you immediately, I would. But I don't know that.

Monday, April 11, 2016

Today we attended a memorial service at Tech, given for those lost this academic year, both students and faculty. The ceremony is called When the Whistle Blows. After words are spoken, and candles were lit, they blew the famous Georgia Tech whistle for each lost one. This was followed by a solemn walk of a portion of the campus.

Mom Mary and Pop came to town for the memorial. The four of us were there, as well as Ibrahim, Uncle David, Greg Abbott, and Hannah. Your dad invited Hannah; I didn't want her there. For whatever reason, your dad wants to keep a connection with her. I would be happy to never see nor hear from her again.

We asked Ibrahim to light the candle in your honor. What a sweet, unassuming kid he is. He told us he may change his major and won't take classes this summer. He is in contact with Dhroov, who is with his family in India. He said that Dhroov is having a tough time dealing with your death and that he had subsequently tried to kill himself but was stopped by family.

Several Tech staff members—the Dean of Sciences, the Dean of the Physics Department, The Dean of Student Life, the Provost, and the University President—were in attendance. All had such beautiful things to say about your mind and your character. Five faculty/staff members died this scholastic year. You were the only student remembered at this ceremony. Dean Stein told me, however, just in these past two weeks, Georgia Tech had lost three more students. Two to suicide. They will be memorialized at next year's ceremony.

I read a passage today that stated if you lose someone as close as a child, you die a bit yourself. A part of me has perished; mostly it's the part that contains the memories and inside jokes that only you and I shared. Those were our stories. Another part of me that died when you did are the thoughts and excitement about your future. Never did anyone believe in you more. I walk around feeling like a significant part of my body has been severed. There is nothing nor no one who can make me a whole person again.

I'm not just marking time until my own death. I have your sisters. And they need me, I hope. Perhaps I've always over-estimated my importance to my children, husband, friends; and yet, you underestimated yours. What could I have done differently to make you feel worthier, more loved? Could we hit the reset button, My Love?

Friday, April 15, 2016

I am still waiting on the acceptance portion of grief. Anytime that I hear a thumping bass in a car, I immediately think it is you pulling into our driveway. You were so loved.

I wish you had thought of us more before you ended your life. Did you really understand what you would be doing to us? Did you care? We are all so sad, not just your family, but also your friends. My sweet baby boy, I will always love you and I know you were suffering from the illness of depression. But I was here. I could have helped more. Please come back to me.

Friday, April 22, 2016

Sam, this is going to come out wrong, but there is a part of me that is mad at you. What the hell? You may have thought you had it rough, but really? Compared to whom? You had parents who would do anything for you, friends who esteemed you, a future which was limitless.

Honestly, of all the 20-year-olds out there, you had such a minimal reason to end your life. You could have made a difference in this world. But beyond that, you have changed the lives of all those who've loved you. I will honor your life by living and being a better person than I was before. But I'd also easily die to bring you back.

Friday, April 29, 2016

Here is a grain of wisdom I just learned from my psychiatrist Dr. Z.: Society needs to change the mindset that boys are not allowed to show emotions. One reason we are losing many of our sons and husbands and fathers is because they have kept things bottled up their entire lives, until they ultimately explode violently.

Monday, May 2, 2016

Today I had a panic attack. Maggie needed a ride to work and I was first trying to get something done for my job, when suddenly my chest tightened, I felt light-headed, and I could breathe only shallow breaths. I looked up the symptoms on WebMD and the instruction was to get to an emergency room right away. I called Jeff and told him I thought I was having a heart attack. He rushed home. While waiting I had the thought that, yes, you can die of a broken heart. Jeff took me to Gwinnett Medical. After an EKG and a blood test and a ridiculously long wait, they assured me my heart was fine. And, indeed the pain had stopped. I was encouraged to see a cardiologist and made an appointment.

Wednesday, May 4, 2016

I feel like a prisoner serving a life term. I just want to check off the days and be done. I have no sadness about the passage of time. All my days seem the same. My only goal is to get to the end of one, so that I can make my tick mark on the prison wall.

Thursday, May 5, 2016

I saw a cardiologist today. I underwent a stress test and an echocardio-gram. All is well with me physically. At least now I know what a panic attack feels like and won't rush to the hospital the next time. Last week I saw my psychiatrist and she said I am likely to have another because of my intense grief. She prescribed Ativan to take when a panic attack seems to be coming.

Saturday, May 14, 2016

Sam, when you told me when we were admitting you into the hospital that I was the one who needed help, you were right. I am getting that help now. Through therapy and self-reflection, I've come to realize how much my anger toward Dad affected you and your sisters. And, to what end? Did I really think I was going to mold him into a new person?

Through traditional and Cognitive Behavioral Therapy, I am realizing my trigger points and curbing my thoughts before they become words. Even a layman psychologist knows that it is really my own insecurity which has caused me to lash out at him all these years.

I apologize to you for the times I tried to seek out your alliance when I was angry with Dad. That was wrong of me. You will be happy to know that I am much kinder to him now.

You were so good, not because of me, but rather, in spite of me. You came into this world kind, you lived a life of kindness, and you left—still compassionate and kind. I love you, I miss you, and I long for the time when we can be reunited.

CHAPTER 24

Seeking Help

In late April, the associate pastor at our church, Jodi, approached Jeff and me in the hallway on Sunday after the service and told us about the formation of a grief support group that she would be leading. Jeff and I said we would give it a try. The support group was set to last for six sessions, meeting on Monday evenings.

The first session would be my last.

The meeting took place in one of the church's classrooms. Our church had been added onto in a series of somewhat haphazard additions, over the years, as the congregation had grown. The classrooms were down a long hallway at the back of the building, in one of the older parts of the church. When we arrived, Jodi had already pulled the chairs in the classroom around to make a circle. I remember it struck me how different she looked out of her official robes and in regular clothes. Jeff and I took our seats. We were among some of the first to arrive, but eventually, seven others joined our group. I noticed immediately that they were all older adults.

As each told his or her story of losing a loved one, I found myself becoming increasingly shaky and emotional. When the circle came to him, Jeff said, "We lost our son two months ago, and so we are still struggling with that."

I looked at him disbelievingly. *Really, that's all he has to say about our loss?* When it was my turn to speak, I shared the background on Sam's depression and subsequent suicide. I tried to convey how important and vital he had been to our lives, how his loss had devastated us. I dissolved into sobs as I spoke.

While I was speaking, Jeff poked me in my upper arm. I looked at him and got the message. I said to the group, "Sorry if I took too much time."

Each person there assured me I hadn't. Jeff was silent. The group members were sympathetic and supportive; still, I could not make it through the remainder of the hour-long session. I excused myself to the hallway outside of the classroom. On the drive home, I asked Jeff why he had poked me. "You were embarrassing me," he said. "No one else was carrying on like that."

I was stunned. "Of course not," I responded. "Most were elderly women who had lost their elderly husbands after long illnesses. No one else had lost their child. And, not one had a tragedy as recent as ours."

We spent the rest of the car ride in silence. Although Jeff completed the six group sessions, I never returned.

Something similar occurred when we attended a suicide survivors' meeting sponsored by the Link Counseling Center, a nonprofit formed by Georgia resident Iris Bolton after she had lost her own son to suicide. Although the center itself is in Dunwoody, Georgia, there was a meeting being held not far from us at Gwinnett Medical Center.

During the first session, Jeff was again hypersensitive to my weepy contribution to the group. He later told me that he was sorry, but it made him uncomfortable to have that kind of attention on him. We had approached Sam's illness differently, and it seemed we would approach his death differently, too. I wished for Jeff to be able to share what was in his heart; his closedness made it harder for me to heal. But I had no more control over Jeff's way of grieving than he had over mine. I decided instead that I would no longer do therapy sessions with him. I needed room to grieve in my own way, and perhaps he needed room to grieve in his.

BACK IN 1998, when Sam was two and before Maggie and Claire were born, Jeff and I saw a therapist for couple's counseling. Jeff became resistant to the sessions, but I continued to see Dr. F. until 2003. The week after Sam's death, I called him. He remembered me and had even seen Sam's obituary in the *Atlanta Journal Constitution*. We made an appointment for me to come see him that same week. That first appointment, all I could do was sob. Dr. F. kept telling me to breathe. For several months, I continued to see him weekly. I have tremendous respect for Dr. F. and know that he helped me navigate that first year of grief.

Besides individual and group therapy, I also started seeing a psychiatrist. She weaned me off the Ambien and Klonopin that I'd been taking since Sam's death and started me on a healthier antidepressant prescription protocol. Without her intervention, I cannot imagine that I would have survived.

The girls were also seeing a therapist, a grief counselor named Holly, whom we did a few family sessions with. Holly has an empathetic nature that the girls readily responded to, but as time went on, Maggie became resistant to continuing therapy. I found a new psychologist for her, but after three sessions, she refused to go back. As my doctor said, I could make her go, but if she was just going to sit there with her arms crossed and her mind resistant, I was throwing money away. Claire was more receptive to therapy and continued longer.

I worried about both my girls to the point of unquenchable anxiety. When they were at school, I sometimes looked around their rooms, looking for any signs of their own emotional distress. I'm not proud of it, but I did the deed most despised by teens: I snooped in their diaries. My need to protect them was unyielding.

On the day after Sam died, Maggie wrote the following entry in her diary:

Dear Diary,

On February 26, 2016, Sam has died. He was depressed. He went missing, and the police found him dead. He hanged himself. My brother, Sam, who I love more than anything has died.

I can no longer ask for help with my math homework or for any advice because he is dead. He left me. I'm not sure if anything will ever be the same again. I guess not. I should have hugged him more. I should have talked to him.

Family from everywhere is coming to the funeral. My friends keep texting if I'm okay. Of course, I'm not, but can I really say that to them?

After what had happened on December 18, he PROMISED he would tell us if he started feeling bad. He LIED. He didn't say a thing. We all thought he was getting better. We all thought everything was going to be okay. They say when depressed people plan their suicide, they get happier because they're so relieved. Maybe he planned it.

I miss him. Every memory I have—he's in it. I just want him to tell me it's going to be okay. I just want him to come home. He can't though, and I'm not sure if I will ever be okay with that.

I'm so pissed that he would do this to us. That he would leave like it's nothing. Everyone is being so nice, but I have no idea what to say to them.

I pray Sam is in heaven. He never wanted to hurt anyone in his whole life, so I know if there is a heaven, he's there.

Claire journaled on the family computer and then printed this document. I found the pages in her bedroom, stapled together. As I read them, my heart heaved for Claire.

5/28/16 Claire Owen Journal about Sam and Grieving

I lost my brother, Sam Owen, on February 25, 2016. He suffered from depression. I was and still currently am 13 years old. A lot of adults don't think that we teenagers know what is going on and they think we are just hopeless/clueless. Although I don't completely understand what exactly death is, I know that it is probably the worst thing that has ever happened in my life and it makes you think: if I'm only 13, my life is going to suck.

Although my therapist thinks this is the worst thing I will ever go through, I don't know my future. I could lose my entire family tomorrow, but let's hope not. It has only been three months and every day is so hard. I always think about "my firsts." I call them "my firsts" because I do things for the first time without Sam. For example, about a month ago my sister, Maggie, had her first piano recital without Sam being there. Then, last Thursday, I had my first swim meet without Sam. Adults think that going out and doing things with others will make things better. I literally just read an article that said that during children's grieving they will want to be alone.

I think my parents are too quick to assume about things. Yesterday, I went to my neighbor David's graduation party. David is 2 years younger than Sam. They were friends as kids, but sadly kind of drifted apart. I was over at their house, and I saw a picture of Sam, and I just felt like leaving, but, of course, I stayed to not seem rude. I understand that society thinks that grieving only takes like a week, but grieving takes years. Let me repeat that YEARS! Not one year, many.

I don't cry all that often as much as I did before, but there are days where I can't even stop crying. Like today, I was looking through Sam's phone, that I knew would make me cry, but I ran into his notes, and there was one note labeled "Things to Tell my Sisters." I read it and just started bawling. It was so hard to read because I didn't know that he would care that much about us to do that for us. After I read it, I realized that he had already told us most of those things. I don't know why I'm taking this so hard, but I just wanted to say that.

Sometimes I wonder if I'll ever see him again, and it scares me thinking I won't. If I were dead and a ghost and realized that I couldn't see Sam, I would die again. Every now and then, I feel like it was my fault that Sam died. I gave him such a hard time because I hated him doing drugs.

I felt fairly suicidal for like a week because I missed him so much. Sometimes, I will have a short panic attack because I feel like I don't remember what he looks like. The only thing I can ever think to tell Sam is that I love him, and I miss him because we only had such a great relationship with each other.

Sometimes I just feel so lonely. Like I feel like I can't even connect with my family. Sam and I were so alike, but of course, he had the good grades.

I feel like I need to hide my feelings. I remember during the first week I was back at school, I had started crying in Social Studies, and I know the teacher saw me. I'm sure my face was red, but he never acknowledged me or asked if I needed the restroom.

I know life is not fair, but I didn't realize it was this unfair.

I understand that hundreds of thousands of people die a day like 12 people die every 6 seconds. But we're the family that would never expect it to happen to them.

I remember that day Sam was missing. I got home around 1:30, it was an early release day, Thursday. I was sitting on the front stairs with our cat, Goose, then went upstairs with her to take pictures with my phone. The last noise that I heard from Sam was the front door closing, hard. All I remember hearing was that. The worst sound I have ever heard in my life, and the last one from Sam.

I also remember the next day when Sam was still missing. I walked in the front door after getting off the bus and talking to Abby and looking at Mom's and Maggie's faces and knew it was about Sam. Mom walked up to me and told me that Sam had died.

About 30 minutes later, Dad called the police department to find out how Sam had died. He hung up, and Mom asked, and Dad said, "He hung himself." My heart dropped. I had thought life was over. But I know that someday I will be able to find happiness and live my not so great life again.

Reading the unfiltered heartbreak from Maggie and Claire hit me hard. They had been given a rotten, rotten deal. I found myself doubting that I was adequately helping the girls with their grief. I needed to do more. I also felt angry at Sam for doing this to his sisters, who adored him. Hadn't he realized how much they loved and depended on him?

CHAPTER 25

Religion and Spirituality

"A great religion is one that creates the deepest peace."

—BENJAMIN FRANKLIN

Before Sam's death, my beliefs about life after death were confused and varied. Starting in my mid-thirties, I began having a hard time reconciling a traditional Christian faith of Heaven and Hell with my knowledge that every religion and sect had such different ideas of how one gets into one or the other.

I was mostly sure, and still am, that the idea of a hell built specifically for non-believers does not make sense. How does one account for an illiterate person in a poverty-stricken, non-Christian country who dies an early death from starvation? Does this hell on Earth equate to Hell itself? By Christianity's terms, this person would be counted as an unbeliever even though no one had ever mentioned Jesus to him. Likewise, how to account for a serial murderer on death row who at the last moment before execution professes himself a believer? A monster who has killed innocents goes right up to share space with the angels?

I was also resistant to Jeff's spiritual outlook. After his dad died in 2005, he began an earnest search into life after death. He gained great peace about death when he first discovered books about the afterlife. He read about near-death experiences, reincarnation, and clairvoyance. He was especially interested in the American philosopher and self-described clairvoyant Edgar Cayce. But when Jeff would try to tell me about the things he was studying, I brushed him aside. I felt his beliefs were too far out of the mainstream.

I have long believed in God and the presence of the Holy Spirit. But I have yet to find an organized religion that rings completely true to me. I have spent many hours of my life listening to sermons that left me feeling bored, restless, and no closer to God. Yet I can go on a hike in nature and be totally enveloped in the presence of God.

MY INTRODUCTION INTO faith as a child most certainly differs from what most people experience now in church. I grew up in a rural town in west Tennessee with a population of around 5,000 people. Although there was only one elementary, one middle, and one high school, there were many churches. The mainstream churches were First Baptist, First Methodist, and First Presbyterian, but there were all sorts of other denominations there. The church my family attended was a small country parish, a Missionary Baptist church. The congregation peaked at around 150 people, many of whom I was related to in some way.

As a child, I never looked forward to Sundays. I would always be made to wear a dress or skirt accompanied by fold-over lacy socks and Mary Janes or, when older, hateful pantyhose. I still remember sitting on the hard wooden pews, tugging at the hem of my skirt to try to cover my knees. I felt as confined as a figure in a coloring book.

The first hour of the church service was Sunday School. We were sorted by age group and sent to small classrooms. The preschoolers went to a room behind the pulpit, where crayons and coloring pages were the main medium. There were other separate classrooms for elementary-, middle-, and high-school-aged kids. The adults stayed in the sanctuary for their Sunday School lesson. Everyone was given a Sunday School book containing the lessons for a quarter of the year. At the end of each season, we would be given a new one.

In the classrooms, we sat on chairs with our Bible and Sunday School book on our knees and took turns reading the lesson aloud—I was always nervous about this, afraid I would read too slow or mispronounce something. We also worked to memorize the order of books of both the Old and New Testaments; to this day, I can recite the names of the first half of the Old Testament books. My memory fails me at *Ecclesiastes*.

After the Sunday School hour, everyone returned to the sanctuary, where it was time for the second hour of church—preaching. The sermons were rarely comforting. The content was always hellfire and brimstone.

I didn't enjoy Sundays, but what I dreaded most was Revival Week. Revival was held once a year during the third week of July and always encompassed my birthday. The event started on Sunday and went on daily with both morning and evening services until the following Sunday. The goal of a revival? To save the Lost.

Revival was like a regular Sunday service on steroids. The feeling of tension at each of those ten services was palpable. My mother did not work outside of the home, so my siblings and I were there for every single service. No excuses, however clever they might be, were ever entertained by our parents. One of the precious few weeks of summer vacation, ruined by the proselytizing of certain damnation unless you were "born again."

While writing this book, I found the tenets of the church from the church association's website. Reading it now, I can see why as a child I thought getting into Heaven was so hard.

> *To obtain true salvation, there first must be a sense of trouble, conviction, and condemnation set up by God in the heart of the unsaved person. They must pray and seek God and repent of their sins until they know for themselves that God has forgiven and saved them. Man does not convict them, and man cannot tell them when God forgives and saves them.*
>
> *God is all-powerful and can save the soul of one seeking Him any place, any time when God's conditions are met. However, we give an opportunity for those desiring to seek and find God to come to the front for prayer. The pew sitting in the front facing the congregation is referred to as the "mourner's bench." The*

unsaved person does not obtain salvation simply by "accepting,"
"believing," "making a decision for Christ," or "being baptized"
as many teach today.
  We do pray with the person seeking God, and we do believe in
encouraging them according to the leadership of the Holy Spirit.
When God saves the individual, the individual knows, without
anyone telling them—including the preacher, loved ones, or any
friend.

In my memory, a morning "Revival Meeting" would go something like this: My siblings and I, along with Mom, would get to the
church a few minutes before 10:00 a.m. The weather was always
sweltering these mornings, making walking into the overly air-
conditioned sanctuary an unpleasant shock. For thirty minutes or
so, we would sing songs—this was the most pleasant part of the
service, but also a time full of dread of what was to come.

The preacher would then take his place at the pulpit. Over the
years, the preachers varied, but one thing that never changed was
the cadence of the sermons. The preacher would start out in a calm
voice, reading a few verses from the New Testament. He then would
put down his Bible and begin freestyling a sermon. Gradually, his
voice became louder, until there was a crescendo of shouting. He
called the "unsaved" corrupt for not heeding the Word of God and
seeking salvation, and I would sink, filled with unmeasurable guilt
for not being good enough for God to save.

Being "saved" or "born again" was a terribly confusing concept
for a child. Believing in Jesus and God, making responsible life decisions, and doing for others was not enough to get you into Heaven.
I was taught that unless you had a mystical experience during which
God would tell you that you were saved, upon death you would be
plunged into Hell—a fiery inferno ruled by Satan. Although I willed
it to happen and prayed as well as I could, salvation eluded me.

After his ear-shattering sermon, the preacher gave an altar call.
This was the point at which every young person in the building would

begin to cringe and divert his or her eyes. Occasionally, some "lost soul" would make his way to the altar on his own. Mostly, the good ladies of the church would walk over and place their bone-chilling hands on us. One might whisper, "Nina, have you been saved?" I would say I didn't think so. I had yet to hear God's voice giving me the "get out of Hell free card."

The congregant would beg me to let her escort me to the Mourner's Bench—a bench placed at the pulpit, facing the pews. Generally, I declined the offer, but occasionally, overcome by fear of Hell, I would acquiesce. The preacher and others would kneel around me, begging God for my salvation. There would be tears and tissues as I asked God to save me. Some of the members stayed in the pews, and others would crowd around me, praying in desperate tones. Smelling the overwhelming combination of floral perfume and stale breath around me, I felt reduced to a spectacle.

Finally, whether or not the "mourner" had been saved, the preacher would end the service, announcing that he would continue in prayer for the lost soul and that we would reconvene that evening for the 7:00 p.m. service.

If one of my siblings or I had been at the altar that morning, the car ride home was always silent except for some sniffling. If all of us had circumvented the altar call, the sense of escaping unscathed was such a relief that we would sometimes be giddy—generally due to my brother, Rusty, saying something silly to lighten the mood. Church seemed removed and alien, as though that was not part of our real life.

WHEN I WAS sixteen, however, I did indeed have a numinous experience inside this church. During an evening service in the summer, while the congregation was singing, I had a spiritual awakening of sorts. I felt myself go into a peaceful state, and an overwhelming feeling of calm washed over me. As shy as I was, I felt confident enough to immediately stand and then walk to the front of the church and tell the congregation that they no longer had to worry about my soul. I knew at that moment that I was safe and that I would not be condemned and sent to Hell.

This is an experience I have never been able to fully explain. As uncomfortable and often torturous as my church experience was, I do feel like my soul ascended to a higher plane on that day. I believe the Holy Spirit came to me as I sat on a back pew and that I was indeed "saved." But, I believe, so are we all. There is no condemnation in death. Some of us will need a lot of ministering in the afterlife, but God and Jesus are love.

As an adult, the harshness of my fundamentalist church up-bringing has stayed with me. To this day, I have inordinate anxiety inside most church sanctuaries, experiencing the beginnings of a fight-or-flight response nearly as soon as I'm inside. Rather than concentrate on the sermon, I either look out a window or look around at the people in the congregation, focusing on clothes and hairstyles—I must distract myself to keep from fleeing. When a service ends, I typically hurry toward the nearest exit. Emotionally, church still makes me feel like that girl in pantyhose being held against her will.

Even so, after Sam was born, I wanted him to experience a church community. I'm not sure why, really. I think that I believed you had to model that for your kid. Like going to school and being a good citizen, or like working hard? Church was just part of the equation.

When I first approached Jeff about going to church, he had no desire. I remember him telling me, "I grew up not going to church and I turned out fine." I promised we'd try to find something that made us both comfortable. We chose a small nondenominational church near our home. The atmosphere of this church was so welcoming and casual and non-threatening that I was able to attend services there and even teach Sunday School to the young kids. Jeff liked the members of the congregation and became all in. He even sang in the choir and worked the sound board. He loved being a part of this particular church community.

We continued attending this church until just before Maggie was born. At that time, we had moved from Alpharetta to Suwanee, and the 35-minute commute was too long to continue attending there. We visited several churches around our new home, but Jeff and I would immediately recoil at anything that hinted at heavy-handed religious proselytization.

We eventually joined Pleasant Hill Presbyterian Church. Jeff and I love the minister, Pastor Dave—the same minister who gave Sam's eulogy. He is a wise man and delivers his sermons in a compassionate, friendly, and genuine manner. I don't recall any sermon given by Pastor Dave with Hell as the topic. Attending this church, my anxiety was still present, but much abated.

The years passed, and our kids—as they entered their own teenage years—attended church sporadically. I, too, became an infrequent attendee. If Sunday provided an opportunity to go for a run or to play tennis, I always chose the outdoor activity. Jeff continued to go to church regularly.

Since Sam's funeral was held at Pleasant Hill, I have become an even more sporadic attendee. I cannot help but see his coffin in the apse of the church. I cannot help but remember the eulogy and hymns rendered for Sam. I can't stop myself from crying while there.

These days, I rarely attend church. I contend that I can better explore my spirituality in nature—God's world. Jeff and I sometimes hike in the Elachee nature preserve or go kayaking at Lake Lanier. While there, while I am quiet, I take deep, cleansing breaths. I close my eyes and can sense Sam and God around me. The magnificence of nature brings me solace and hope.

CHAPTER 26

Signs, Signs, Everywhere a Sign

One thing I have learned since Sam died is that life is so much more than we can see. Brokenness cannot be made unbroken, but it can evolve into something new. Hope, perhaps?

The first time I became aware of Sam's presence after his death was the day after his funeral. I have often worn his Burberry watch since his death. The watch is classic in design, with a black leather strap and a round face. It was a gift to him from us for his eighteenth birthday.

On March 2, 2016, I was sitting alone in my bedroom, wearing the watch. I was crying and telling Sam how much I missed him. Suddenly, I got a distinct vibration on my wrist. I was puzzled, thinking for a second that I had my Fitbit on. I looked at my wrist and realized the sensation was coming from his watch. It felt like the vibration you get when you've achieved your step goal, but subtler and longer-lasting. I explored the watch carefully, and there was no alarm setting on it. Although startled, I felt comforted, wondering if Sam was trying to communicate with me. I had not expected to receive signs from Sam after he died. Before his death, I had doubted that the dead could communicate with the living. But this felt real somehow and couldn't be logically explained.

The watch vibration occurrence happened several other times over the first year after his death, and not only when I was alone. I have experienced it when riding in Jeff's car with him, when home, and when out in public.

I don't wear Sam's watch much anymore. The strap is getting worn, and I don't want to ever replace the same strap that touched his skin. However, there are days that I do put it on—generally his birthday or an anniversary—and some of these times, I still get that vibration. I have no doubt that it's a sign from Sam.

A FEW WEEKS after the first watch event, I was lying on my bed, turned onto my right side. It was morning, but I didn't feel up to facing the day yet. I felt my mattress shift, as though someone had suddenly sat on the far back corner of it. I looked over, expecting to see Jeff sitting on the bed, tying his shoes, but no one was there. I looked around the room, but there was no sign of a person or a pet.

I felt unnerved but closed my eyes to see if it would happen again. It did! I continued to lie there, feeling the energy become a warmth over my feet. Sam was with me.

This beautiful sign still comes to me, although not as frequently as it did the first year after his death. When it does, I feel nothing but reassurance. I continue to lie on my side, a smile on my face, and appreciate the presence of Sam.

On March 7, about a week after his funeral, Sam came to me for the first time in a dream. When the dream happened, I was sleeping in his basement bedroom. I had been spending a lot of time there, wanting to be surrounded by his things, trying to get as close to his physical presence as I could. In the dream, he appeared as though floating above me. I could only see his face and upper torso. He was dressed in a black t-shirt with an open red plaid button-down over the tee. I don't recall him owning these specific clothes, but they were something he probably would have worn. He looked directly at me, twisted his mouth in a wry manner, and said to me, "I'm sorry." I've seen Sam make that exact face dozens of times. It was his way of being self-deprecating, but also being real. He was saying that he had screwed up by killing himself and he was very sorry for doing this thing to our family, maybe especially to me.

This was more than a dream. This was Sam. Upon waking, I felt a stabbing pain, but also a small amount of relief that Sam was reaching out to me from the Beyond. I thought he must be doing okay if he was able to do this. It was the moment when I first began trying to forgive him. He could not have comprehended how his action would forever change each of us.

A COUPLE OF months later, I was having lunch with my friend Tricia. She had lost her dad about ten years before. During lunch, she asked me if I had seen a lot of cardinals since Sam had died. I told her I hadn't really noticed. As we were finishing our meal, she emailed me an article claiming that a cardinal is a representative of a loved one who has passed. When you see one, it means your loved one has sent this sign to you. They usually show up when you most need the loved one or miss them.

The next day was Saturday. Like all Saturdays, Angela and I went in the morning to the greenway for a run. We were at the beginning of the trail and still walking when, out of nowhere, a male cardinal flew onto the path a few feet in front of us. It turned its head and looked directly at Angela and me for a few seconds. I stopped dead in my tracks. *Amazing.* "That's a sign from Sam," I told Angela. I explained what Tricia had told me, and Angela agreed that the way the bird had appeared was both unusual and meaningful. That was my first sighting; cardinals would become my frequent visitors over the next several months.

Just days after this significant cardinal sighting, I was revisiting some belongings when I found the Mother's Day card Sam had given me the previous May, my last Mother's Day card from him. The message on the cover said, "A good mom knows when to let her children spread their wings and fly." Beneath it was an unmistakably cardinal-like red bird.

I'm not one to collect greeting cards. But I did keep this one, probably because Sam had written a sweet note inside the card, saying he loved me and appreciated everything that I had done and continued to do for him.

Up to that point, I had vaguely thought about getting a tattoo to honor Sam, in part because I had given him such a hard time when he'd gotten his. This card was my inspiration. It took me months to go through with it, but in August, I went to Killer Ink in Buford with three friends and got my first-ever tattoo on my left wrist: Sam's signature copied from the card.

Not for one moment have I regretted getting my one and only tattoo at age 50. The copy of Sam's signature is a constant source of comfort and a reminder that Sam does indeed love me.

AT THE BEGINNING of August, Maggie needed a ride to school for a meeting. School was starting in a few days, and she was going into her junior year. I was having one of those days where the sadness over losing Sam was especially poignant, and as I drove home after dropping Maggie off, I began to cry. I had been told of a heart-linking technique, putting a hand over one's heart and talking directly and out loud to the deceased loved one.

In the car, still driving, I began speaking to Sam. I was crying hard and said, "Sam, I just cannot go on without you. I cannot do it. This is too hard. I miss you. I know you want me to be strong for the girls, but I can't be. You are ever-present in my mind, and the regret and sadness are always there."

I came to a red light. I was at the crossing of Lawrenceville-Suwanee Road and Peachtree Industrial Boulevard. I sat at the light, my hand on my heart and tears streaming down my face. Across the intersection, a pickup truck pulling a trailer turned left in front of me. Emblazoned on the trailer were the words **"There's Hope."** I gaped; small bumps rose across my body. A rare smile emerged. I had an immediate sense of peace come over me. Sam was answering me—he was telling me that there is hope!

After arriving home, I googled the phrase and could only find a religious organization named There's Hope based in Kentucky. (I also found a site for a local organization that was titled There's Hope

for the Hungry, but the logo was different from the one I had seen.)
I had never seen a truck trailer like this before and have not seen
one since. The truck was placed in my sight by God—I felt certain.
I was crying and talking directly to Sam, stopped at a red light, and
saying I had run out of energy to push on, and that truck and trailer
turned left straight in front of me. Sam was saying, "Mom, you can
push on. There's hope."

A few weeks later, Sam came to me in another dream. He was
floating above me as he had in the previous dream. He asked me to
please stop focusing so much on him and to turn that focus and love
to Jeff and the girls and to myself. His appearance was somewhat hazy
in this dream, but his voice was clear. There was an aura around him.

The next morning, I told Jeff of the dream. His response: "That's
good advice from Sam."

IN OCTOBER, WE went to Gulf Shores for the Columbus Day weekend. The girls had Friday and Monday off from school. Since Sam
had died, I had often made plans for us to go out of town, to be places
where no one else knew our story. We were on the last hour of the
six-hour trip, and I was driving. It was dark out, and I was thinking
of Sam and asking him to help me be more kind and patient with
our family. A distinct star appeared directly in my view, out the front
windshield. The crazy thing was that no matter whether I turned
right or left, the star stayed in my direct vision for almost twenty
minutes. Not only that, but it was the only star visible in the night sky.

Jeff was snoozing, and I poked him and asked, "Do you see that
star?" He picked up his phone and used an app and said the star
was not actually a star, but the planet Saturn. I felt it was Sam telling
me he was near and would not desert us. Some astrologists refer to
Saturn as the "Guardian of the Threshold" because it's the farthest
planet that is visible in the night sky to the naked eye. It has been said
by some that it is a symbol of someone who has learned what he can
from life on Earth and is now entering the realm of what is beyond.

Sam has been so present in my healing. The image of Saturn took on a beautiful shape as I looked at it, perhaps because of my tired eyes. When we arrived at the beach house, I drew a picture of the shape:

I've often wondered if this symbol stands for anything. I shared it with my friend Rebecca, who said, "It looks like an A. It looks like a mountain peak. It also looks like the tip of an iceberg. There is so much more to reality than we can see or know."

WHILE ON THIS same vacation in October, I was told of a beautiful tribute to Sam's memory. My friend Michele is the mother of one of Sam's best friends, Jackson. She texted me to tell me that four of Sam's best friends, including Jackson, had got tattoos in his honor. Sam's friend texted me pictures of the ink.

Two of the boys had got tattoos with Sam's name and birth and death years. The other two had replicated the tattoo that Sam had had: "I've made a few bad decisions."

After finding out about the tattoos, I sent a group text to all four boys telling them that I had also gotten a tattoo and shared the text conversation that Sam and I had had about his tattoo.

> **Me:** *I just learned of the beautiful gesture you all made by getting tattoos in remembrance of Sam. I am so full of love for all of you, and I can promise you that Sam knows about this and is feeling such love for you all. I've had many signs and dreams from him, and his energy and spirit are still with us.*

Adam: *Thank you for sharing that with us. I for one know that I am leap with the tattoo that I got, and think it is a great way to remember him by. We all miss him so much, and whenever we all see each other, the conversations always wrap back around to Sam. I think that text exchange between you and Sam when he got his tattoo does a great job of capturing his personality, I couldn't help but start laughing when I read it. Again, we are all always here if you or your family need anything.*

Will: *Sam had such a huge effect on all of us that we wanted to commemorate his life while also making sure that we always remembered the impact that he had on all of us. I'm sure he was looking down and smiling while you were getting your tattoo and I hope he knows how much we love and miss him.*

Jackson: *Honestly, I don't even know how to put my feelings into words. I think about Sam every day. I have so many memories of him that it seems like everything I do reminds me of how much I miss him. Whenever we all see each other and reminisce about fun times that we have had, every single one of those memories involves Sam doing something hilarious that makes every one of us burst out laughing. I'm glad we did this to commemorate him. He is ever present in our thoughts and in our hearts. We all miss him so much.*

Michael: *Like all of us have said, not a day goes by that I have not thought of Sam. He will forever be on my back like a hand on my shoulder. I just hope he found peace in the end because I too have had dreams of him.*

These texts renewed my pride in Sam. He must have been a good, important friend for these guys to get tattoos specifically honoring him. I felt love and appreciation for these young men, and I believed Sam did, too.

From my journal—10/16/16

I dreamt of Sam last night. He wanted to go to Wisconsin to visit graduate schools. He was considering Marquette and another school that sounded something like Columbus, also in Wisconsin. In the dream, I wanted to use my Delta voucher and miles and go with him, but he wanted Jeff to go instead. I was disappointed but felt like he was doing well. I woke up thinking the suicide was the dream, but then a second later realized that in fact the suicide was our reality and I felt crushed. I sleep so much because that is the only time that I get any sense of peace. My reality is my nightmare.

I composed this journal entry six days before Sam's twenty-first birthday, on October 22. It was unimaginable that we would have to face Sam's birthday without him. The night before his birthday, I was again sleeping in his bed in the basement. I had gotten up at 3:30 a.m. to let our cat, Goose, inside. Goose is an indoor cat but had run outside earlier in the evening. I had been worried about her and had prayed she wouldn't run off or die on Sam's birthday.

After getting Goose safely inside, I climbed back into bed and fell asleep. As I slept, Sam came to me in a dream. In the dream, Jeff and I visited Sam in the afterlife. Sam was living in a dorm-like facility, with a single window in the room and something resembling metal bunkbeds. The room was not very big and had hard laminate floors.

Sam seemed physically unchanged. His mood was solemn. I asked if I could hold him and he said okay. I sat on the floor, and he sat next to but facing me. I cradled his upper body. It felt wonderful to touch his live body—he was no longer the stiff mannequin that had lain in the coffin. Jeff stood beside us. We asked Sam how he was doing, and he looked at me and said, "I cannot move forward to the next tier of the afterlife until you forgive me for the suicide."

I looked into his eyes and told him I forgave him. He seemed uncertain, but I continued to reassure him. Sam said he continued to feel so sorry and guilty for what he'd put us through.

We asked him what his days were like, and he told us he was studying alternative medicine at a school in Indiana. (Not sure how that works, but since this ws the second time in one week I'd dreamed of him studying and learning, I believe that is part of the afterlife experience.) He told us one fact he has learned is that we should all be vegetarians and never eat meat.

Next, I asked if he ever saw anyone in the afterlife he'd known before, and he said, "Granddaddy and Granny." Granddaddy was my maternal grandfather, and Granny was his mother, my great-grandmother. Sam had never known either of them; I fleetingly wondered how he would have recognized them. I asked how they were, and he said they were often sitting in rocking chairs beside one another and bickering back and forth. This bickering described their relationship in this world, too. My grandfather was Granny's only child, and she had often chided him well into adulthood.

I asked Sam if there was anyone else, and he mentioned a guy from high school he'd known and a couple of other people. He told us that one guy there was mourning being in the "godless afterlife," but Sam had encouraged the guy to look up to the light above and all around. Sam told him, "That is God, and He's present."

Sam had told us he was doing a sport that involved pushing large sleds (like football players practice with) with a team and then climbing up and down obstacles. Jeff said, "You sound like you really enjoy that." Sam said he did. Then we all stood and looked out the window, and Sam pointed to a field where we could see others engaging in this sport.

Sam said that when he'd first gotten to the Other Side, they had done a full physical on him and uncovered that he'd suffered from MS while here on Earth. We wondered why no doctor here had diagnosed him.

Then, it seemed, the three of us all sensed it was time to part. We told Sam goodbye and that we loved him. Then I said, "We'll see you soon." Sam hugged us and said he loved us too.

The parting was sad, yet in the same way, a tremendous relief. I woke from this dream with a light heart for the first time since Sam's death. I felt peace.

I went upstairs and found Jeff in the kitchen. I told him about the dream. He said that he had read that it is possible to visit the afterlife, that others have recorded such events, but that it was rare to do so. I picked up my phone and, in the notes section, wrote every detail of the dream that I could remember. I had real proof of my son's current life, and no one can tell me that this was not an actual visitation with my son. This dream also shifted something in me so that I could finally forgive him. It felt like a chunk of a boulder had fallen away from my chest.

LEADING UP TO Sam's birthday, Jeff and I had tossed around several ideas for how to mark the day. At one point, we wanted to have extended family and maybe friends over to have a celebration of Sam's life on his birthday. But as the day came closer, I had a panic attack, my second since Sam's death. My psychiatrist gave me some good advice in saying that it was not my responsibility to heal my extended family or friends. That my duty was to help heal my two girls and myself, and that was it. She did not think hosting a big gathering on Sam's birthday was a good idea. Jeff and the girls and I agreed to celebrate/acknowledge/memorialize Sam's birthday by spending the day together, just the four of us.

Thank goodness I took my doctor's advice. Otherwise, I wonder if I would have been in the peaceful state that had allowed me to visit Sam in the afterlife and to have another remarkable experience.

Jeff, the girls, and I planned to visit the Botanical Gardens in Gainesville to memorialize the day. We took Interstate 985; I was driving, Jeff was in the passenger seat, and Maggie and Claire were in the back of the car. The day was windy. Out of nowhere, a blue plastic bag blew right in front of our windshield. There was nothing on the bag except a white S.

"Did you see that?" I asked Jeff.

"Yeah, what was that, 'Super Bag' [as in Superman]?"

"No, that was from Sam," I said. "He was telling us that he will be spending his birthday with us."

This bag genuinely seemed to come from the Beyond. We didn't see any car or truck it could have blown from. We could think of no place of business that used blue plastic shopping bags with only a white S on them.

The Gardens were peaceful and not crowded, and we saw many unusual varieties of butterflies that morning. At some point, we began to trade funny stories about Sam. Claire shared that when she had been little, she had fallen asleep on the bottom bunk of Sam's bunkbed. As a brotherly prank, Sam drew on her face in marker. When she woke up, she looked in the mirror and was quite upset. She said she remembers telling Sam: "Why would you use my face when you had a coloring book on the floor in your room?"

We left the Botanical Gardens and drove to a casual seafood restaurant in Flowery Branch. Sam had liked seafood. Driving there, we were on a remote two-lane road. To my left was a row of houses. The houses had nothing on their doors for decoration, save for one, which sported a large silver scripted S. He was still with us.

Sam's birthday was the first day I started noticing the Ss. They continued to show up, often in the most unexpected places. I've been hesitant to talk about or show these Ss, as I realize they could be conceived of as being contrived. You'll have to take my word for it that they weren't.

One day I was in my friend Amy's car. We were going shopping. I noticed something on my sunglass lens and removed the glasses to wipe them. When I took them off, there was a hair from our Great Pyrenees in the form of a perfect S. Another time, I was cleaning the kitchen. We'd had spaghetti for dinner, and everyone else had left the kitchen. I was wiping up the counters and the stovetop. I stopped in mid-wipe: on the stovetop was a random piece of pasta formed into an S.

There were other instances of Ss besides these, such as a piece of dental floss found on the floor and an S initial carved into concrete. I can't recall all the Ss and cardinals that came my way. Because they were so frequent, I tended to not document every sighting. Still, I was always happy with either sign. These moments of happiness generally lasted a day. The next day, I would often be plunged back into despair.

In November, Sam once again came to me in a dream. He spoke directly to me and said, "Mom, I am not my death. Please stop focusing on that and on the regret that it encompasses. The twenty years that I lived on Earth are full of so many better, impactful memories. Please try to think of that when you think of me. Every time you go directly to the day in February when I died, or the day after or the days before, you make me feel such guilt. This change in your thought process is a part of the forgiveness I am asking you for." When I woke, I had twinges of guilt. Sam was calling me out on my constant mind loop focusing on the days around his death. I knew I needed to make a concerted effort to push that aside and start focusing on the many good memories I had of Sam.

One day in mid-December, while alone in the house, I kept hearing chords being played. Some seemed to be played on a guitar and others on an organ or piano. Of course, I searched for the source but did not find one. The chords sounded four times during the day. That same day, in the evening, I was alone in our basement watching television and noticed a photo on the wall rocking back and forth. No air was blowing near it, and although the photograph was among many other framed ones in a photo montage, this was the only one that rocked. It was a picture from the Hall of Mirrors at Versailles, from the time I had gone to France with Sam.

Throughout December, I dreaded Christmas. We all did. I could not fathom the pain of celebrating at home as we always have. I did not want to put up a tree with the ornaments we had collected as a family; I did not want to hang stockings without hanging Sam's. I just couldn't.

After talking about the beach or the mountains, we decided we would spend the holiday with my parents in Tennessee. I thought being with family would help us get through this Christmas. I knew my extended family would be gentle and supportive. While there on Christmas Eve, I asked everyone if they would join me in lofting remembrance balloons in honor of Sam. I had bought a pack of biodegradable balloons for Sam's birthday two months before, but we had never used them.

We stood around the kitchen table as my siblings, parents, nephews, and nieces each selected a balloon on which to write a message to or note of remembrance of Sam. Then, the group of us went outside. The night sky was cloudy, and there was a strong wind blowing. As we lit the balloons with a lighter and attempted to loft them, they collided with the wind, and many fell to the ground. One landed in the lot across the street and started a small fire (which we were, thankfully, able to put out). The one I lofted, however, stayed in the air. It traveled up and across the dark sky until drifting out of sight.

Afterward, back in the house, I felt particularly teary and melancholy. I said goodnight to everyone and went to my room. Lying in bed, I had the familiar sense of Sam's energy, the same unmistakable weight on the mattress, that I had experienced months earlier, after his memorial. I said a little prayer: "Thank you, God, for letting Sam come to comfort me this Christmas Eve."

On January 12, 2017, I began working on this book. The project seemed overwhelming, but I also felt a calling to complete a book about Sam. I downloaded Scrivener and began to organize my journals and notes and Sam's written materials. That afternoon, I stood up from my computer and chair to look out of the window. There was a baby cardinal in the grass. I watched it for a while, and then it flew into the bush.

The little guy was mostly brown with a red beak and some red on his tail. I wasn't entirely sure it was a cardinal, so I took a picture and then googled it. It was indeed a baby cardinal! I believe this was Sam telling me two things. One, he had begun a new phase in the afterlife, and two, he was telling me it was time to give birth to this new project—my book.

I NOW CALL October 22 through February 25 the *Season of Suck*. In this time period, we have Sam's birthday, the holidays, and then the anniversary of his death. I knew the weekend of the first anniversary of Sam's death would be hard. To get through it, Jeff and I retreated to the mountains of north Georgia. We rented a yurt in Cloudland Canyon State Park. It was just the two of us. Claire attended a church retreat with a friend that weekend, and Maggie worked and hung out with her friend Elena.

Being in nature at the state park, I could feel Sam's presence. I felt at peace and knew that he was with us. Jeff and I had quiet conversations about Sam and spirituality. I leaned hard on Jeff to get me through this hateful anniversary. Our marriage had become neither significantly stronger nor weaker than it had been before Sam had died. To this day, we are still trying to figure out where our marriage goes from here. I can't say specifically if we are closer or farther apart, only that we are different. But that weekend, I felt close to Jeff.

In March, I had another dream. In it, Sam and I were sitting together on a steep hill. Other people were sledding down the side of the hill, but it wasn't icy. Instead, the mound was covered with a beautiful grass of Irish green.

Sam told me that three other people had died by suicide the same day he had, but he went on to say that he was the only one who had made it "back." He immediately started to correct himself by saying, "Well, not really back…"

I stopped him mid-sentence and said, "No, you have made it back. You are with me now, and your spirit is with me continuously." The dream (or my memory of it) ended there.

That same day, I went running on the greenway with Angela. During our conversation, she told me that our mutual friend, Peg, knew of a family who had lost their son by suicide a few weeks earlier, on February 25—exactly one year, to the day, after Sam had died. I thought of how, in my dream, Sam had told me of three others who had died the same day. I realized he had said "day" specifically, not "date." I wondered if this boy could be one of the "others" he had spoken of.

Later in March, I was given the opportunity for some part-time contract work with a virtual hotel sales and service company. The job amounted to only 15–20 hours per week but would keep me occupied for a portion of each day and would allow me to work from home. I had quit my previous full-time job in October because the stress had been impeding my healing. But, with no work, I needed a distraction from my thoughts. I took the position.

On March 28, I spoke with Christy, a company manager, who said she had an additional opportunity for me. The conversation eventually turned to our personal lives.

Although Christy lived in Orlando, we learned we had both lived in Memphis for significant parts of our lives. We had other things in common, too. At one point, she said, "I was looking at your resume and see that you live in Suwanee. I have a cousin who lives there."

"Really, what neighborhood?" I asked.

She said she wasn't sure, but her cousin has twin girls who went to North Gwinnett High School and graduated in 2014. It was not only the same school Sam had graduated from, but the same year.

A light bulb went off for me. Christy's last name is a bit unusual, and I realized I knew those twins. In fact, Sam had taken one of the twins on a couple of dates, and the other twin had been part of Sam's French class trip to Forbach, France. Over the years, he had had several classes with both girls.

I said to Christy, "I know those girls!" I then told her of our tragedy, and she said she remembered when Sam had died. She said the twins had been shocked and very sad about his death.

Sam had graduated with more than 600 classmates, and I knew only a fraction of them. For me to have known of these girls, and for me to be given an opportunity to earn more money for the family while not increasing my hours, seemed more than a mere coincidence. My angel was by my side and helping me.

Once again, I said, "Thanks, Sam."

Later that same week, I went to the grocery store. While this might sound like a trivial activity, since Sam's death, I'd suffered from pangs of agoraphobia when forced to go to places alone. I found it easier to just stay at home and let Jeff pick up what we needed.

On this day, I went to the Fresh Market nearby and bought a few things. When I returned home, I walked into my kitchen and saw feathers strewn on my countertop. I recognized them as the mottled feathers of a young cardinal. I looked for Goose, thinking if she had killed a cardinal, that would be the end of her. But, instead of the cat with a dead cardinal, I found Goose in our family room, sporting a death stare aimed at the top of our two-story windows. There on the ledge sat a young male cardinal, alive but looking terrified.

Trembling, I herded Goose and our dog into the basement. I needed the bird to survive. I called Jeff and asked what I should do. He said I should get a broom and hold it bristle-side up near the bird, and the bird might hop onto it, and then I could put it outside.

I tried to follow Jeff's advice, but I was shaking so much that the bird would not light on the broom. That was when Maggie came in from school. She took the broom from me and held it up toward the bird. The bird immediately hopped onto the broom, and together, Maggie and I walked out onto our deck, and the bird flew away and lit on a tree branch—unharmed.

Some people have said to me, "Oh, I've had a bird come into my house before." But this was a young male cardinal. I have no idea how he got into the house. No door was ajar. And he survived a cunning cat. It was Sam sending another cardinal to make a personal visit. He also left a tangible gift—the feathers. I sent love and thanks to Sam for this blessing.

I kept the feathers. Others confirmed that the photo I had taken of the bird was the profile of a cardinal and that the feathers were those of a young male.

NOT ALL SIGNS have been as dramatic as the cardinal in my home; others have been subtler. One such incident happened on June 9, 2017. I was again shopping at Fresh Market. (This store is manageable for me because it is small and rarely crowded.) This day, there were only a handful of customers in the store, maybe ten or twelve other than me, and all were women. Passing between aisles, I smelled the unmistakable scent of Sam's cologne, YSL Libre Homme. I looked all around, but there was no one near me or in either aisle. I also looked for a man working in that part of the store, but there was none. I turned my cart around, back to the same spot, and the whiff of his cologne was gone.

Hannah had taken Sam's bottle of the cologne, but I had purchased one for myself after he'd died. I know that scent well and was happy to have this special sign.

When Sam was young, he loved birds of prey. We would take him to falcon shows at the Renaissance Festival and at Callaway Gardens or to Reelfoot Lake to see the eagles there. He loved to read about these fascinating creatures, and when he was little, he would watch nature videos on birds of prey over and over. He could cite from memory different characteristics of different birds, including wingspan and speed of flight.

One day that August, Claire and I were home alone together. I was in my office, and she came running to me, saying there was a hawk on the railing of our screened-in porch. I went outside and saw that there, indeed, sat this majestic bird on a small rail outside the screen of our porch. It stayed there for over a minute, letting us take pictures.

I don't know if it is unusual to have a hawk light on a ledge so close to people. Regardless, another fascinating and appropriate sign from Sam. According to legend, the hawk is a messenger bird. Usually, when we see a hawk, it means to pay attention because a message is coming to you. Hawks represent clear-sightedness, being observant, and guardianship. They also bring courage, wisdom, illumination, creativity, and truth. Hawks give us the ability to see the larger picture in life. They can help one to overcome problems and make wise use of opportunities.

Just a few months before Sam died, he and I had a conversation about books. A love of books was something Sam and I had in common. Sam asked me if I knew what his favorite book was, and I said *The Catcher in the Rye*. He said that had used to be his favorite, but after reading Donna Tartt's *The Goldfinch,* that had become his favorite novel. This made me happy. I had also loved reading *The Goldfinch* and had encouraged Sam to read it, as a main theme of the novel is the coming-of-age story of a young man.

On October 22, 2018, to acknowledge what would have been Sam's 23rd birthday, Jeff and I went to Yonah Mountain for a hike. As we were starting our trek at the base of the mountain, a bright yellow bird appeared out of nowhere, lighting on a nearby bush and staring directly at us. I gasped a little and asked Jeff what kind of bird it was.

"It's an American Goldfinch. It's rare to just see one male by himself. They are usually in pairs, and you generally see them at suet feeders."

Chills ran up my body. I knew this was a sign from Sam and that he was again with us on his birthday.

A good mom
knows when
to let her children
spread their
own wings and fly.

Sorry I've been so difficult these past couple of weeks. I'll try harder to stay busy and out of your nerves. Just know that I love you and appreciate all you have done (and continue to do) for me.

Enjoy your day off! God knows you deserve it!

Love,
Sam

Mother's Day card from Sam to Nina, 2015

Love,
Sam

Nina's tattoo

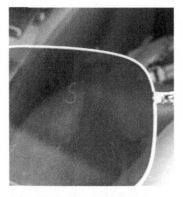

A few of the Ss Nina recorded

Young male cardinal on the second-story window of Nina's living room

Cardinal feathers Nina found in the kitchen

Hawk on Nina's screened-in porch

CHAPTER 27

Carol and Kellen

In October 2016, I was working out with my friend Erica in her home gym. Erica is both my friend and my trainer. As we exercised, she mentioned that she knew a family from her girls' soccer team who had just lost their son to suicide the week before. Erica told me that our stories were similar and asked whether she could give the mom, Carol, my name and email address or phone number. I told Erica to maybe wait a little while. In my experience, in the early days, I had not been in a position to absorb anything, much less to hear of another tragedy or to take advice from a stranger. I didn't tell Erica this, but I also wasn't sure I felt up to being in the role of consoler; it had only been eight months since we'd lost Sam.

Five months later, at another workout session, Erica again brought up this family. It was now March 2017. Erica told me that the boy's name was Kellen and that he had been an 18-year-old student at Georgia State University. He was the family's oldest son. Erica had been right; there did seem to be similarities in our tragedies. I told her she could pass on my information and that I would wait for Carol to reach out.

Three more months passed, and in June, Carol called me. At first, I did not make the connection about who she was, but it soon became clear. I remember feeling nervous as we talked—afraid to say the wrong thing. During my grief I had learned that there is nothing someone can say to you to make you feel better, but there are many things people say that make it worse. I didn't want to make her grief worse. I also wasn't sure I was ready to listen to the story of another tragedy.

Our phone conversation was stilted. It was as though neither of us was fully ready to dive into our stories—not just yet. We only talked for about ten minutes, but we made plans for brunch a few days later, on June 20.

That first get-together, we met at Another Broken Egg Café. Because Carol didn't have any social media accounts, I had no idea what she looked like. Over the phone, she had told me she had auburn hair with bangs—all the details I had to go on. I spotted her as soon as I walked in, standing in the alcove of the restaurant. She had a pair of blue wayfarers perched on top of her head and was wearing a blue tie-dyed tee-shirt. Her auburn hair was dyed ombré. Unlike me, she looked like the cool, fun mom.

At the table, Carol gave me a generous smile. She did not seem to be nervous or shy. She asked about our story. I told her my oft-recited speech of what had happened to Sam. She nodded sympathetically as I spoke.

Next, I asked Carol about her own story. Kellen was her oldest of four children, a bright boy who had had much promise. She said that before his death, they had had no idea that Kellen had been depressed, that he had hidden it well. In one way, that made me sad for her. At least we had known of Sam's illness for six months and had tried to help him. In another way, I envied her. Wouldn't I have preferred those last six months without the constant sickness of worry?

As Carol told her story, much about her felt familiar. The faraway look in her eyes was the same look I saw in the mirror. There was a sadness that remained on her face even when a smile came, a polite gesture that never reached her eyes. What showed in her eyes was also in my soul. A vacancy left by the horrible, irrefutable loss of a child. The light that should be there, the one that connects one's soul to one's eyes, had vanished for us both.

The brunch was pleasant, but I walked away thinking how much energy it would cost me to start a new friendship. Especially given that our main commonality was tragic loss.

Even so, a week or so later, I called Carol to see if she wanted to go to The Link with me to attend a suicide survivors' support session. I had told her about the organization when we'd met, and she'd seemed interested. Carol told me she had a conflict with the date. I asked her about the following month's meeting, and she seemed unsure. I was beginning to think she didn't want to pursue a friendship. I didn't press her further. We didn't communicate again until four months later.

ON THE EVENING of October 17, my phone buzzed. It was Carol texting to say I had been on her mind lately and she was wondering how I was doing. I told her I was having a tough time—Sam's twenty-second birthday, October 22, was the coming Sunday. Carol had not known when Sam's birthday was, but she said she was also struggling because the first anniversary of Kellen's death was in three days, on October 20. I hadn't known what date Kellen had died, and the coincidence surprised me.

We made plans to meet for lunch at Maverick's Cantina, a Mexican restaurant not far from where we had met the first time, on Tuesday, October 24, but Carol later had to cancel because her kids had an all-day cross-country meet. We rescheduled for that Monday, October 23. I canceled that meeting, telling Carol that I wasn't feeling well. Finally, on October 27, we met. That lunch was the beginning of a heaven-inspired connection.

Carol told me that she had felt compelled to contact me. She hadn't realized it was Sam's birthday week, and I hadn't realized it was Kellen's "angel-versary." During our lunch, we discovered that we both had attended the same college, the University of Memphis. I have no recollection of ever meeting another person in Atlanta who had attended my school. Not only that, but we were there at the same time. I attended the school from 1984—1988, and Carol attended from 1985—1989. I was in the journalism program, and Carol received her B.S. in psychology and then went on to get a master's degree to teach.

Carol and I talked about our children and found that our youngest children are the same age and Maggie is a year in between Carol's sons. We started talking about people we might both know from Memphis. She mentioned her friend Annette, who was in the journalism program two years behind me. We must have worked on the school newspaper, *The Helmsman*, together at some point. I couldn't remember Annette by name, so Carol began to describe her to me, looking on her phone for a picture. At that exact moment, Annette's husband walked into the restaurant with a colleague. Carol's mouth fell open. He came over to our table to say hi. Carol told the man about the shocking "coincidence" of just then talking about his wife. He showed me Annette's picture on his phone. I felt pretty sure we had crossed paths at school.

Whereas the conversation at Another Broken Egg had been a bit stilted, this time, we never ran out of things to talk about. We talked about how hard it is to maintain a life for the children we have on this Earth, how hard the holidays and birthdays are, how both of our husbands seemingly busied away their grief. We talked about the wrong things people say and how some friends and family no longer know how to act when around you. I left that two-hour lunch feeling awed and inspired and excited about our new connection.

The next Friday, my friend Amy and I went shopping at two home décor outlets in Roswell. We shopped for a couple of hours without much success before going to get some lunch. I suggested the Avalon in Alpharetta, an upscale outdoor shopping center with several good restaurants. I drove us to the shopping center and asked Amy what restaurant she wanted to go to. She suggested a seafood restaurant, Brine. I hadn't been there before, but it sounded fine to me. As we walked through the restaurant's patio to go inside, I heard someone shout my name. I thought, *I know that voice. But from where?* It was Carol with a group of friends.

I walked over to her, and we were both shaking. To run into one another in a place not near where either of us live or frequent could not be a coincidence. Neither Carol nor I had ever been to

Brine. This had to be Kellen and Sam in Heaven placing us together, probably saying, "Look, Moms, you guys need each other. Who else can better understand what you are going through?"

I can't emphasize enough how amazing this encounter was. I had been telling Amy in the car about my recent lunch with Carol and our many things in common. I also had told her about the surprise of Annette's husband walking into the restaurant at the exact moment we had been talking about her.

At Brine, Carol and I introduced our friends to one another. Both of us felt that running into one another so soon and so randomly could not be just a coincidence. Something or someone else was at work here.

Carol texted me that evening, "It was so cool to see you today! I'm still a little shell-shocked! I think you're meant to be my friend, so maybe after Thanksgiving, we can have lunch again. But if I randomly run into you before that, be forewarned that I just might faint!"

I replied, "It was incredible running into you today! I was almost shaking when I saw you. This was no coincidence, and no one can convince me that it was."

After this meeting, we did have lunch with Annette and had fun talking about Memphis. I took a leap of faith and told Annette and Carol the story about the trailer reading "There's Hope" while I had been talking to Sam. They looked at one another and nodded with smiles.

"We believe that, too," Carol said. "For me, one way that Kellen communicates is by leaving quarters in various unexpected places. I always find them when I am feeling down or thinking about him. He also comes to me in dragonflies."

FROM THAT POINT on, Carol and I began to meet for lunch on a monthly basis. Each time we spoke, we uncovered more parallels between our lives. We spoke openly about our spiritual evolutions—our dreams and our visions, our visitations from our sons.

I could hardly believe that our newfound spiritual beliefs mirrored one another's. Carol had also been raised in a traditional Protestant church, but since Kellen's death, she had started seeking more clarity. I've thought since about how grief changes you. How do you go back to worshipping God in the same way when He so clearly let you down? Grief makes you seek a more coherent view of an afterlife. The vagueness that I harbored from my Christianity was not enough. And it wasn't enough for Carol.

December 1 was Kellen's birthday. I bought a Christmas ornament for Carol that said, "I have an angel in heaven. I call him my son." I drove to her house and just placed it in her mailbox. I wanted to let her know I was thinking of her that day.

When Carol texted to thank me, she told me about a charity where she volunteers that serves foster children in the state of Georgia. She explained the duties to me and told me about a day recently when she had had to choose from the gently used donated clothes for a three-year-old boy. She'd picked out a jacket and found the name "Kellen" written on the tag. I told her I was happy he had been there with her, doing volunteer work that mattered.

After our conversation, I felt moved to volunteer there, as well. Just as Sam had found a sense of purpose through charity work, I knew it would be the same for me. I needed to do something to put my life in perspective. I was not the only one who had suffered loss; many of the foster children had lost parents due to addiction issues or death. My first day was Tuesday, December 19, 2017. Since I wasn't familiar with the location, Carol and I met at an agreed-upon spot so that I could follow her to the center. When we met, Carol said she had a gift for me. She handed me a giftbag that contained a beautiful piece of three-dimensional artwork with an angel. On the back, the artist had written the word "Hope." Carol said she'd wanted to give me something that evoked hope because she remembered my story about the truck and trailer that had read "There's Hope."

As we stood there in the parking lot, she said, "You're going to laugh at me if I tell you what my first instinct of a gift for you was."

"No, I won't. What?"

"A poster or a DVD of the Star Wars movie, *Episode IV—A New Hope.*"

She asked me if Sam had been into Star Wars. I said that he had, and in fact, on his last Christmas, he and I had gone together to see the latest Star Wars movie, *The Force Awakens,* during the afternoon on Christmas Day. It had been the first Star Wars film released in seven years. Carol and I both marveled at this nudge from Sam. She said she had felt a strong impulse to buy the Star Wars item but would have felt silly if the instinct had been wrong.

That evening, I continued to think about Carol's instinct about Star Wars. As I folded laundry on the floor of my bedroom, I recalled that when Sam had been young, he had loved everything Star Wars, especially Lego kits. Most of our Legos had been given away, but I remembered that we did have one intact Lego kit still and that it was on a shelf in Sam's childhood bedroom. I knew it had a Star Wars theme but wasn't sure which one. I wondered whether the kit would have the word "hope" on it.

I walked down the hall to the bedroom and opened his closet. I had to stand on my tiptoes to reach the box. I pulled it down and placed it on the bed. The cover was dusty. I brushed off the dust and saw that it was the Millennium Falcon. I didn't see anything with the word "hope" on the lid of the box. However, the Millennium Falcon did first appear in the *A New Hope* movie.

I sat down on the bed and opened the cover. Inside the box, besides the Legos, was the folder containing Sam's senior letters. I was stunned. I had been looking for those letters since Sam had died and had finally given up, thinking he had thrown them away. When Sam had graduated in 2014, I had wanted to read his letters, but he hadn't wanted me to. He must have stuck them in that Lego box then.

I immediately called Carol to tell her the story. She was delighted. She said she knew that instinct was strong. We both were thankful Sam had whispered Star Wars into her ear. The letters were a Christmas miracle, a gift from Sam to me. I read the sweet and encouraging and complimentary letters that friends and family (including my grandmother at age 93) had written to my son. I was filled with renewed pride in him.

To this day, Carol and I are uncovering new parallels in our lives. There are too many to list here, but most importantly, she is one of the few people to whom I can openly talk about my spiritual communication with Sam. She has the same with Kellen. If Carol and I had never met, I do not think I would be as far along as I am now in dealing with the loss of Sam. There is no doubt that knowing Carol and working through our grief together has helped my healing. I no longer feel so alone in my sadness. I am certain that Sam and Kellen, through God, have brought us together. I am blessed by this friendship.

CHAPTER 28

Mediumship

A few weeks after Sam's death, Jeff scheduled a session for himself with Brad, the reiki master and hypnotherapist Sam had seen. Jeff said he wanted to talk to Brad about Sam's last session with him, which had occurred the week Sam had died. When Jeff told me about the appointment, I said I thought it was a waste of time. I told him that Brad had obviously done nothing to help Sam, so what was the point?

Nevertheless, when Jeff returned home, I asked him about the session. Before the appointment, Brad had not known about Sam's death. Jeff said that Brad had been shocked and saddened to hear about our loss. Brad had known from meeting with Sam that he had been emotionally burdened, but he had not thought Sam had been suicidal. Jeff said he asked Brad if he had any mediumship ability and if he could communicate with Sam. Brad explained that his ability in this field was limited but recommended a medium named Chris who lived in North Carolina and did readings over the phone.

Jeff told me he was going to set up a phone session with this medium.

"Are you out of your mind?" I asked him. "Do you really believe that there are people who can connect with the dead?"

He said he did. I told him to keep me out of it.

Even before Sam died, I knew Jeff was interested in mediumship. In the years just before Sam's death, there would be times where Jeff encouraged me to have a past-life regression session with a spiritual healer. I had resisted, feeling it was another sign of the ways Jeff was always trying to fix me.

At this time, I didn't believe in reincarnation, and I certainly didn't believe in mediumship. I thought it was all bonkers. I told Jeff, "Of course, Chris will have researched Sam and us to the nth. His obituary and much more are easily found online."

"I don't think so," Jeff told me. "Anyway, what could it hurt?"

THIS BACK-AND-FORTH CONVERSATION was typical of how Jeff and I were communicating in the early months after Sam's death. I did not feel supported by him. He would sometimes find me alone, crying, and would say, "What are you upset about? I mean besides Sam?" It was always Sam. I could tell Jeff wanted to normalize things as much as possible for our daughters. I could not imagine returning to normal.

A month or so after Sam's death, I remember sitting with Jeff, watching television, when he let out a sudden and uproarious laugh at something on the show. I was stunned. How could he possibly laugh and not feel immersed in grief and guilt? It took me many months before I could laugh without guilt.

I mostly cried to and confided in close friends and family rather than Jeff. When I did try to talk to him, he would listen and then offer advice. I did not want advice. There was no solution to the devastation I felt. To our friends, neighbors, and family, Jeff seemed largely unchanged. He was still jovial, in fact. I could not wrap my head around this, but I also knew that I could not be the one to make him mourn appropriately. I deeply resented his quick reset to normal. I thought the only explanation was that he wasn't experiencing the same level of grief as I was.

So, when Jeff set up the first session with Chris in January 2017, I stayed upstairs while Jeff took the call in the downstairs office. Although Chris's fee was nominal, I hurt too much to listen to someone trivializing my son's death to make money.

Jeff recorded the conversation using his phone. The call lasted an hour. Immediately after the call, Jeff typed up notes on the computer.

He tried to tell me about it, but I was resistant. Although he printed out the notes and left them on the computer desk, I avoided them for a few days. One day, however, when he was at work and the girls were at school, I read his notes.

- *Sam's soul popped right up when Chris went looking for him. His first comments were that he did not mean to hurt anyone when he left. He hated how he made us feel when he left. He knows his actions have changed our lives forever.*
- *Sam's soul is currently getting the extra help he needs to keep learning, growing, and evolving spiritually. When we cross over with certain problems, they go with us into the afterlife where they are easier to treat. Sam came into the world as a troubled soul. He is an old soul who got tired in this lifetime and wanted to go home.*
- *I told Sam I felt we had let him down, but Sam said no one is to blame for his leaving early. The decision to leave came from inside Sam.*
- *Sam has nothing but love for all of us. Chris said this was unusual because most suicides have anger toward people in the world, particularly family members.*
- *During Sam's time on earth he was very empathic. He picked up on the feelings of others easily. This caused him a great deal of worry and was a reason he left this world early. He said he got tired of other people's crap (constantly feeling their problems due to his empathic nature).*
- *Given the state of his soul coming into this world, it is amazing that he made it to adulthood. This was due in a large part to the love and support of his family and friends.*
- *Twenty years does not sound like a long time, but Sam said the fact we kept him here until he was an adult is a very big deal. This was repeated a couple times. Sam said his soul evolved and learned a lot in the years he spent with us.*
- *Heart-linking technique. Put hand on heart like in pledge of allegiance and think about Sam. Talk to him silently or out loud. He will hear us.*

- Sam is always around us. The best thing we can do for Sam (or anyone else that has passed) is to keep praying for his soul to evolve, learn, and advance because our souls are always growing – even after we leave this earth.
- Remember the good times about Sam, not when he was depressed or ill. Keep talking to Sam; he hears everything we say to him. He misses being with our family. He is still here – we just can't see him.
- Try to push away feelings of pity or anger – they don't help. Try to laugh and think of the good times with Sam. Chris said Nina is drowning in her grief.
- I asked about Sam's drug use and if it was a factor in his suicide. Sam said it was not a factor in him committing suicide and that it may have helped him gain insight. (That sounds like Sam....)
- I asked if spirits really do visit in dreams. Chris said yes, they do. She also said when we are asleep our subconscious mind travels the world. Sometimes we meet unsavory spirits and sometimes we meet friendly spirits. She said that if we had bad dreams of Sam, they were not from Sam, God, or the Light. Sam would only have good things to say if he was contacting us. Be aware there are malevolent spirits out there that will want to mess with you.

Although I had picked up the notes doubtfully, as I read, I began to feel like maybe there was something to this. Besides revealing things about Sam, Jeff's notes also showed aspects of his own grief that I had not realized. I didn't know that Jeff thought we had let Sam down. In our conversations together, Jeff and I would say we had done all we'd known to do to save him.

The stuff about Sam being an empath and an old soul are things I'd always thought about him. Because I didn't really believe in reincarnation, I was not sure what I had meant by calling Sam an old soul when he had been a child, but he had always had a calmness and wisdom that were beyond his years.

Claire also read the notes and expressed to Jeff that she wanted to participate the next time so she could talk with Sam. She did participate in the next session and seemed relieved and happy after it. When I asked her if she believed what Chris said was true, Claire said, "I sure hope so!"

Over the next year, Jeff had two more sessions with Chris. I would listen in on part of the calls or listen to the recordings afterward, but I was not convinced that she really was communicating with Sam. I thought some of the things Chris said were too general, and not necessarily specific to Sam. I wanted to believe, but I held back. *Do reasonable people believe in mediums?* I wondered.

I couldn't be annoyed at Jeff for spending money on the sessions with Chris because he paid for it out of his own account. We've always had his, hers, and ours banking accounts. Chris's fee for a session was only $50. Jeff had openly listened to me when I'd described my dreams and signs; maybe mediumship was the only way for him to connect with Sam, I thought. He claims to never remember his dreams, and he isn't observant of things going on around him. Without saying much about it to Jeff, I began to open a little window of belief inside myself that maybe mediumship was real.

One day while having lunch with Carol at a Tex-Mex restaurant near my house, I brought up Jeff's exploration of mediumship. She and I had talked often about our signs and dreams but had never broached the subject of mediums or psychics. But for some reason, on this day, I shared Jeff's belief in mediums. Carol immediately became animated. She said she wholeheartedly believed in mediumship and felt she had a gift of clairsentience, herself. She told me that my vivid dreams and visions could indicate my own clairvoyance. (I'm still uncertain of this.)

Because of the sense that Carol had had at Christmas about Sam communicating about Star Wars, *A New Hope,* and the wonderful gift of senior letters that had produced, I did not feel shock. In fact, I felt relieved. *Really, there is someone else who feels like their loved one is connecting with them through a medium?* As we talked, I began to believe more fully in the possibility of mediumship. I was more receptive to Carol than I had been to Jeff when we'd first discussed the topic, but by the time of Carol's and my conversation, I had been toying with a belief in clairvoyance for a few weeks.

Carol told me that even as a child she had believed she had a sixth sense. Through a spooky intuition, she had known things she shouldn't have known and had seen things others hadn't. I asked Carol if she had used a medium to talk to Kellen, and she said she had. The medium she saw was Susan Rushing. Susan worked out of Phoenix and Dragon, a metaphysical bookstore in Sandy Springs, just outside Atlanta. Carol had had an in-person session with Susan and found her insightful.

Carol told me that Susan has written a book called *Suicide from the Other Side*. She suggested I get a copy, and the next week, I did through Amazon.

I didn't start reading the book right away. It sat on the table beside my bed for a month or more. That spring, we took a family trip to St. George Island, Florida, where we rented a house with its own pool. I spent a lot of time beside that pool, reading Susan's book.

Susan had lost her daughter's father to suicide, and she wrote that internal searching, meditation, dozens more suicide readings, and the messages they had delivered had led her to a new way of healing. I was intrigued. Upon returning home from Florida, I called Phoenix and Dragon to make an appointment for an hour session with Susan. I was only asked to give my first name—no other information was required. I eagerly—and anxiously—awaited our meeting.

ON THE DAY of the session, April 11, 2018, I drove into Sandy Springs to the bookstore. I had visited once before with Carol. That first visit had been overwhelming to me—every inch was stacked with books, crystals, candles, and gemstone jewelry. I felt a heady aura filling the store. I seemed a little wired. Carol said that was the power of the crystals and the psychic energy in the place. I wondered if that could be true. I felt far removed from my comfort zone. Even so, the mental energy felt palpable.

This day, I met Susan at the front counter. She escorted me to a small back room. It had little furniture other than a cluttered desk, a desk chair, and a large leather chair that reminded me of the massage chairs you see at malls. There weren't any windows in the room to let in natural light. I felt tongue-tied and nervous.

I'm not sure what I was expecting Susan to look like. Maybe I pictured her with dark hair, black clothes, a little goth-like. But Susan could have been anyone I'd met playing tennis or at school events—she had light auburn hair styled to just below her shoulders and wore a cute top with jeans. She had an effusive smile. I started to relax.

Susan instructed me to sit in the leather chair. She sat in the smaller desk chair, facing me. She asked my first and last names and wrote these on a page of a yellow legal pad. I had brought my own notebook and pen. At the time, I hadn't known if Susan would let me record her. But in general, I feel more connected while writing things down. (Maybe's it's the writer/wannabe journalist in me.) By making my own notes, I could record not only what she was saying, but how I was feeling.

Susan closed her eyes. I watched as her facial expression changed from pleasant to one of concentration. She lifted her hands, palms up, and murmured for her spirit guides to help with my reading. From her book, I already knew that she relied on angels and spirit guides to assist her with her mediumship.

Moments later, Susan blinked her eyes open and began talking to me. She intuited that I had two girls and asked me their names. I told her and she wrote them underneath my name on the legal pad. She said, "I have a strong intuition about Maggie. She is set in her ways. She's the 'queen of reciprocity'—if someone does something for her, she will repay, but likewise, she expects people to do for her if she did something for them." Susan went on to say that Maggie has a beautiful smile and knows how to talk to people. She will be a business whiz and successful in whatever she does. I felt pride for my older daughter and smiled. She had described Maggie perfectly.

Next, she spoke about Claire. Susan said she saw Claire as feminine and nurturing. She said there was something with her back and that we needed to watch this because it could turn into painful arthritis as she ages. Susan could see the "S" in Claire's spine. I was amazed. Claire has scoliosis, and she has both an upper and lower curve in her spine — an S. There was no way Susan could have known this.

Susan closed her eyes again. "I see two people coming forward for you, Nina. The first person is a woman, about 5'2", talkative, blue-eyed, and blond."

I said that description sounded like my recently deceased friend, Shirley, who had died in September 2017 after a long bout with cancer. Susan went on to say that there was a man with her. She described him as tall, and maybe a relative.

"He is very funny," Susan said.

I asked if this could be my son, Sam, and she said no. I felt deflated. In a rush of words, I told her about how I had lost Sam. She offered her condolences, and then said she would have to say a special prayer to her guides and angels to conjure up Sam, because he had died by suicide. She fell silent and once again closed her eyes, lifting her hands, her palms facing up.

Susan opened her eyes and placed her hands in her lap. Sam had appeared to her, she said. Susan described the person Sam had been on Earth as a combination of high anxiety and an outward show of calmness. She said that he'd told her that in life, he'd known profound happiness, but also profound sadness and loneliness. He hadn't been able to see outside of his own vision of himself as a failure. He'd either felt things were perfect or they were completely wrong.

Susan said Sam had a big heart and had been generous on Earth, and gifted, but he had not been able to see those qualities in himself. He'd quickly become disillusioned with the world. She said this was Sam's last time on Earth.

As she spoke, I wrote frantically in my notebook, trying to get everything down. Sam said through Susan that his suicide had been impulsive and not planned. This was what I had long felt, and it reinforced my belief that he could have been saved.

She said he was telling her that he owed a debt to me that he wanted to repay. I wondered aloud about this and said he owed me nothing. But Susan pressed that it was something Sam was clear that he wanted to do. She said it had something to do with lies told to me in my childhood that I still hold onto. Sam felt a debt of gratitude to me for loving him so much, and he wanted to help me reclaim my joy, she said. (Over the months and years following this session, I often wondered what Sam was referring to. I've come to believe that he wanted me to learn how to love without always putting up walls, to stop being afraid of being the one who gets hurt. My insecurity has hampered my ability to show love to others.)

Susan said that in the afterlife, Sam could manipulate things in order to help us much better than he could on Earth.

I asked her if Sam had a message for Claire. Susan saw water with Claire, that she enjoyed the water. (All three of my kids have been swimmers, so this made sense to me.) Susan said that Claire was a healer; her softness was her strength. Sam communicated to Susan that he was worried that Claire would marry too soon and have a child too soon to be able to mother. This would be a mistake, as she has a lot to do as a healer of others.

Sam also said Claire was less savage than Maggie.

I said to Susan, "I don't think Sam would describe Maggie as savage." But Susan was firm that savage was the word Sam used. (Later, after Claire read my notes from this session, I specifically told her to not mention the savage comment to Maggie. I didn't want to hurt Maggie's feelings. Claire told me that the word "savage" today is used as a complement—it means cool, hilarious. I was happy to hear Sam's intended meaning.)

Susan said to me, "Claire needs a lot of sunlight in her life. Vitamin D3 is crucial to her wellbeing. Claire is an empath and even psychic, although she hasn't really uncovered these gifts. She is meant to counsel others. Observe the effect she has on others."

I asked Susan to ask Sam if I should help the girls be more open to the spiritual world, and she said he replied, "No, let them find Jesus on their own."

Through Susan, I asked Sam why Jeff had not had any experiences with Sam's spirit. "Dad prays hard, but almost with closed fists," he replied. Sam said he was sometimes with Jeff on his phone screen. (Susan pantomimed her finger sliding across a screen.) Sam was also with Jeff during his work commute, sitting in the passenger seat, sometimes messing with the radio. He said once, he'd thought Jeff had sensed him and even reached over into the empty seat.

Next, Susan said, "He's telling me to tell you to not miss an opportunity just because we lost him." Wondering if he was referring to the book I had begun to write, I asked if the book was the opportunity he'd mentioned. She said Sam said yes and told me to not get caught up in the wordiness. To write my heart, then go back later to clean up the writing.

Then I asked about Hannah. My anger toward her since Sam's death had been unyielding. I'd wondered often if she was one of the reasons he had killed himself. I thought I might learn something that would help me move forward. Sam's words through Susan: "Hannah metaphorically swims in the shallow end of the pool." Every time Sam had tried to pull her into the deeper end, she had refused. Sam had been sad when he was here because he'd wanted to make a meaningful connection with Hannah, but it had been impossible. Sam said there was no need for us to maintain any connection with her.

I told Susan to ask Sam about the four friends who had gotten tattoos in his honor. Sam said he had been surprised yet moved by the tribute. He had also been surprised at the number of people who had attended the visitation and the funeral. He had not known how much people cared about him, nor how much he would be missed.

Susan could see Sam, and she described him his way: Thin but with broad shoulders. Beautiful eyes. Long eyelashes. Physically, he wasn't finished growing. She described his long arms, with an almost Spider-Man-like quality. Susan had never seen a picture of Sam.

She went on to say that Sam had a beautiful glow to him, like sunshine, but with both gold and silver mixed in. Susan said she wished she could show it to me because he was pure light and beautiful.

Sam had worked extremely hard to get well on the Other Side, Susan told me. He had angel guides, but they did not walk beside him, supporting him; they were behind him. Sam was happy, she said, and helping to heal other people in the afterlife. There was a relative who had shown him the way when he'd first gotten there.

Thinking of Sam's professed atheism, I asked Susan if he had been surprised when he'd awoken on the Other Side. He said he had been most surprised at the expanse of it all. Heaven was the entire universe.

Sam said he had never felt more powerful nor more peaceful. He said the power was in the peace. (Susan said, "Wow, that's profound. I need to write that down." And she did.) He said that he had achieved so much in the afterlife already that anything else is extra credit.

Susan mentioned how fast Sam's mind worked and how she had to concentrate hard to relay everything to me. He had a lot to tell me.

What Sam wanted me to know was this: He had deep gratitude toward me for loving him. His love for me was like the fire of a thousand suns. Sam had me in his hands throughout my way.

He said he was not sorry to be off the Earth, but he was sorry for the damage he'd left behind. When Sam had first gotten to the Other Side, he had been shown the rest of what his life would have been like on Earth, and there would have been more bad events than good. He said there was a glitch in his "brain box" that made him so hard on himself.

Susan saw a dog and described our Sadie perfectly. Then, on her legal pad, she drew an outline of our downstairs and indicated that Sam's spirit would sometimes come in the door from the garage to the kitchen, walk across the family room, and sit in the chair in the corner. He said Sadie sees him. (It's true that more than once I have seen Sadie sit up abruptly and look at this kitchen door. She then wags her tail and moves her gaze toward the family room. Staring for a few seconds at a chair.)

Sam volunteered that he comes to me in things that fly, especially cardinals, because he knows I love color. I felt a wave of validation for my feelings about these birds.

Finally, I asked Susan if I would see Sam when I die. I prayed the answer would be yes. She said I would absolutely see Sam when I cross over. But first, he wanted to help me with the thing that he'd mentioned to make my cross-over easier.

As the session ended, Susan stood. I followed suit. My legs felt shaky; I had tears in my eyes. I thanked her but didn't have adequate words to really tell her how thankful I was.

I walked to my car and drove the twenty-seven miles needed to get me home. The house was empty. I went to my computer and created a new document. In a rush of typing, I transposed my written notes to the document—filling in the details while my memory was fresh. I could not wait to share my experience with Jeff and the girls. I felt so happy and so relieved. It was real. Mediumship was real. Sam was thriving in the afterlife.

A COUPLE OF months after my reading with Susan, I went with Carol to a small group session with a second medium, Amy. We drove together with Carol's friend Lisa on a Saturday morning. I was apprehensive and told Carol as much. Susan's revelations had brought me so much happiness; I could not imagine taking a chance that someone else would give me a dissenting reading.

Amy's office was in a business park in Roswell. There, three other women sat in a room around a rectangular boardroom-style table. All were middle-aged white women. Amy, too, was a middle-aged white woman. There were to be six people plus Amy for the session. Carol, Lisa, and I were the last to arrive. As we sat, Amy introduced herself and told us what to expect.

She said she would try to give each of us a reading, connecting with a dead friend or loved one, but that because this was a group reading, she would not be able to give as much detail as she would in a one-on-one session. She said that we were seeing her at a good time. She was at the height of her mediumship ability now. She explained that clairvoyance was a practice which needed to be learned and honed and the gift was likely to fade as she further aged. Amy described her mediumship as talking to real people on the Other Side. She said she sees, hears, and feels them. Spirits sometimes show her photos or images; it is totally up to them how and if they communicate.

Amy led us into a more informal room in the office suite. The room had a large window overlooking the parking lot of the business park. A sofa and a few chairs were gathered in a lopsided circle. Amy sat in a large green La-Z-Boy-like chair. Carol and I and another woman sat on the sofa, and the others took seats in the chairs.

I knew Amy was for real when we first sat in the room and she said, "I love readings like this. The energy in here seems charged. The next thing you know, a bright red cardinal will fly into the room."

"What made you say that?" I asked.

She said she had no idea. It was just something she felt.

Before she began the readings, Amy instructed us to not tell her anything about who we wanted to connect with. When she said that, I felt tingly and excited. In my session with Susan, I had had to tell her I was there to communicate with Sam; she hadn't automatically intuited that.

Amy regarded the three of us sitting on the sofa. She said she sensed our three lost loves took responsibility for their passing. This turned out to be true not just of Carol and me, but also of the third woman sitting on one end of the sofa.

Amy began the readings with a woman sitting next to her on the left. Because of my nervousness, I didn't pay strict attention to her reading. In fact, I can't recall the details of anyone else's reading.

When it was my turn, I picked up my pen to write notes. Amy said, "Please don't. Let your friend write the notes for you. I want you to be fully engaged." Carol volunteered to be my note-taker.

Amy began by saying that there were two people there to see me. One was a handsome young man. She described him with swept-over brown hair; she said he loved loud music and kept a messy room that had posters in it. She could sense a dry wit and calmness. Sam.

The other person who was there to see me was a woman who had died of cancer, Amy said. She could sense that the woman was a mother. This had to be Shirley again, popping into my reading, as she had with Susan. Amy said they had both died too young.

Shirley's spirit told Amy to tell me that she helped look after Sam now. This comment brought tears to my eyes—in Shirley's final note to me before she'd died, she'd written, "It will be my pleasure to look up Sam when I get there."

Through Amy, Shirley asked that Carol, Lisa, and I go out after the session and raise a toast to her. She said we should not feel sorry for her. Lots of people had cared for her and given her love during her time on Earth. She told me to tell our group of friends that she read everything written for her, and to please change the picture on social media, because it made her look matronly!

As Shirley communicated, Amy said Sam was in the background. He was smoking a cigarette and was impatient for Shirley to finish. Shirley said she would go. She told the group thanks for letting her pop in.

Amy said that as Shirley stepped away, Sam came forward. He appeared with his grandfather and two dogs. Amy described the dogs, and they sounded like two family pets we'd had when Sam had been younger—Abby and Simon. Amy said that Sam told her that sometimes, in the afterlife, he preferred the company of the dogs over the "old people."

Amy told me that when we cross over, we are always greeted with care, support, but also objectivity. When Sam had been shown his life, he had been made to understand that there were other avenues he could have taken to preserve his life. But Sam now had free will, and that meant that he had worked through everything.

Sam told Amy that he knows I talk to him a lot, and he has sent me many signs. Still, he said, it seems like I need a sign from him almost every day. He said that just last week, I had found a penny on the floor and picked it up and wondered if it was a sign and placed it on a brown table. (This happened. The previous Monday, I had seen a penny on the floor and picked it up, but it had been tails side up. I'd wondered about it being a sign but decided it probably wasn't and placed it on our kitchen table.)

Amy conveyed that Sam said he wanted to settle once and for all that it was his actions that had contributed to his passing. We were not responsible. Sam said that he needed us to know that he now realized how good he'd had it — that we'd sacrificed for, put up with, and supported him. Through Amy, he said that he was in a good place with no judgment.

I felt a warmth come over me. Amy paused and smiled. She said, "Your son is standing behind you right now. He just gave you a kiss on the top of your head." She told me that Sam had said something. *"I will never leave my mom's side."*

Afterword

I realize that I may have lost a portion of my readership when I wrote about my newfound spirituality. I understand that my experience of interacting with mediums and seeing signs from beyond will make many uncomfortable. But, by leaving any of these occurrences out, I would be withholding my truth and my spiritual development since Sam's death. I think expanding one's thinking after a tragedy is crucial to surviving and having hope. And, without hope, what is there?

This evolution of my spiritual self has not replaced everything that I believed before. I know God exists, and that He is the Light. When I pray, I pray to God. When I communicate with Sam, I talk to him either in my head or out loud, much as I talked to him here on Earth. Some days, I hear him answer me.

I'd like to share a passage by Maurice Barbanell (1902–1981), an accomplished journalist with parapsychological gifts. This is from his book *They Shall Be Comforted*. His writing largely supports my beliefs.

One day after "death" you will be the same individual as you were one day before it, except that you will have discarded your physical body. You will express yourself through your etheric body, which is a replica of the physical one. It does not, however, reproduce any of its imperfections, including disease and infirmities.

You must try and understand that life in the spirit world is not dreamy or nebulous. It is full of activity. It is just as real as the life that each one of us lives here. We are accustomed to think of the material world as being real and solid, although this is not so, as the science of physics proves. The things of the mind, or the spirit, seem to us shadowy and vague, but to those who live on the Other Side, the mental is the real, and the physical is the shadow.

The spirit world is around us. Some people see it and hear it because they can tune into its vibrations.

The spirit world will not be so unfamiliar as we think because most of us visit in our sleep state. Unfortunately, few of us re-member what transpires. When, however, we pass on, the law of association of ideas will recall our nocturnal experiences.

In many cases, those who die go through a difficult period of stress, due to the fact they cannot reach the ones they love on earth. When they have awakened to an understanding of their new life, they naturally return to their loved ones to tell them of their survival. Be open to this communication and look for signs.

My hope in writing this book is to speak to anyone who is or has been suicidal, or who knows someone who is. I believe my story gives insight into how the taking of one's own life is devastating to family, friends, and community. A needless death leaves a hole, a sadness, a deprivation never to be filled.

I have learned a great deal through my grief and writing about it. One of the things I've learned is that you cannot know peace nor expect others to love you until you love yourself. We are all worthy of love.

The "what ifs" and the "blame game" do nothing to aid in healing after a devastating loss. I've had to learn that I am not in control of anyone other than myself. I've had to learn to give myself a break. Jeff and I did all we knew to do to preserve Sam's life. No family is immune to the tragedy of suicide.

If you see yourself or your child or a friend or an acquaintance exhibit or express suicidal thoughts or actions, please act and seek the very best help you can find. Depression is a horrific disease, never an embarrassment, and it is taking too many of our loved ones. In the

United States, deaths from suicide increased 25 percent from 1999 to 2016. In the same year Sam died, 2016, nearly 45,000 Americans ages ten and older killed themselves.

No one is destined to take his or her own life, and depression and other mental illness can be treated. Never ignore a child or adult who says he or she is contemplating suicide. Even a seemingly offhand remark needs to be taken seriously and addressed immediately.

I have another hope for this book. Regarding faith and the after-life, I hope you will inquire into your long-held doctrine and beliefs and see whether there is room to explore. Certainty is dangerous. It prevents us the freedom of evolving. As theologian Paul Tillich wrote, "The opposite of faith is not doubt, but certainty."

None of us truly knows what happens after we die, or how God works. The divine is vast and beyond our limited understanding. Try to keep an open mind. Read about different faiths. Experiment with meditation. Be accepting of the miracles that nature offers daily. I am proof of the possibility for a spiritual evolution. And it has saved my life.

One thing I ardently believe is that there is life eternal. Our souls never die. Sam's spirit is still with us. Thank God.

Acknowledgments

I started working on *Throwing It All Away* in January 2017, almost a full year from the date of Sam's death. In the year prior, I had regularly journaled about not only my sadness, but also about the miraculous signs I received from Sam. I felt there was a story there that might help others, but it was not until I found Sam's writing that I felt compelled to write this book.

I want to acknowledge Sam's written contributions to the book. Early on, I decided that I would leave Sam's writing verbatim. I felt that doctoring it in any way would mute his voice. I believe that his writing voice describes the inner struggles of depression and drug use that he battled.

In thanking people for their support of this book, I want to start by thanking my family—Jeff, Maggie, and Claire. Even as they were dealing with their own grief, they put up with me during the three-year endeavor I underwent to get the book to a place I could feel proud of. I love them so much.

There are so many people I credit with helping me craft this book. I'll start with the Decatur Writers Studio administration, instructors, and fellow students. Over the last three years, I have participated in several classes and workshops here. The feedback from the instructors and the participants helped me refine my writing. I have learned so much from these classes.

I met my first editor, Lee Ann Pingel, during one of the classes at Decatur Writers Studio. Lee Ann worked with me on two separate drafts of the book. Her guidance, suggestions, and edits refined my writing, and I am extremely grateful to her.

Special thanks to Steve McCondichie with Southern Fried Karma. I first met Steve at the Broadleaf Writers Association annual meeting in September 2019. At the conference, I had a ten-minute meeting with Steve during which I pitched my book to him. After that meeting, I immediately thought, *That's my guy. I'm going to work with him.*

Everyone I worked with at SFK has been professional and supportive. Thanks to Eleanor Burden and Mandi Jourdan for their management and marketing expertise. I want to especially thank Elizabeth Ferris, the editor at SFK. Elizabeth's insight and ideas for the book were instrumental in bringing the book to completion. She is an extremely talented editor. Besides line edits, Elizabeth helped me revise the content and structure of my book. I feel so fortunate to have been given the opportunity to work with her.

I want to thank my friends who read drafts of the book and offered advice — Carol, Angela, Rebecca, Kolinda, Lisa F., and Nancy. I want to thank members of my family and other friends who have tirelessly encouraged me along the way — Mom, Dad, Amanda, John, my late brother Rusty, Lisa N., Carey, Heather, Joseph, Stefanie, Amy, Melissa, Courtney, Sherri, Diane, Liz, Barb, Kyle, Robin, Katie, Erica, Peg, Clare, Tricia, Lisa G., Gail, Susan, Dawn, Christy, Alyson, Patricia, Tasha, Angie, Ron, my late friend Shirley, Anna, Laura, and Beth. You are all terribly important to me.

Finally, I want to thank God for giving me twenty years with Sam. His life profoundly impacted the lives of those who loved him. His memory and spiritual presence live on. I hope this book makes him proud. I love you, Sam.

About the Author

Nina Owen has a Bachelor of Arts degree in Journalism from the University of Memphis. This is Nina's first book. Although writing was her first love, for practicality's sake, her career has been in the hotel industry, where among many other operational and sales tasks, she has been utilized as a content writer. Nina lives in metro Atlanta with her husband, two teenaged daughters, a Great Pyrenees, Sadie, and the family cat, Goose. When not writing, she enjoys playing tennis, hiking, and reading.

Made in the USA
Monee, IL
13 October 2020